The Hero Among Us
FBI Witness Hunter

A Memoir

JIM INGRAM

with James L. Dickerson

SARTORIS
LITERARY
GROUP

A traditional publisher with a non-traditional approach to publishing

SARTORIS LITERARY GROUP
P.O. Box 4185
Brandon, MS 39047
www.sartorisliterary.com

AUTHOR'S NOTE

I worked on this memoir with Jim Ingram right up until his death on August 2, 2009. It was his wish that the book be titled "FBI Witness Hunter," because he felt that was an accurate description of his responsibilities as a Special Agent for the Federal Bureau of Investigation during his 29-year career. However, after writing the book I realized that his contributions to the FBI—indeed, to the United States—were so much more than what that title indicated. So, after consulting with his family, I changed the title with their blessings to *The Hero Among Us*, but kept his original title as the sub-title. Jim Ingram is that most rare of subjects for a writer—a true hero. His dedication to his work is inspiring not just for the effort expended, but for the results of that effort. As Americans, we owe Jim Ingram a great deal. It is my hope that this book does his remarkable career justice

—James L. Dickerson

CONTENTS

To my loving wife, Marie

And our sons, Jim, Stan and Steve,

Of whom I am so proud

INTRODUCTION

By William F. Winter

"Where have all the heroes gone?"

That was a question posed to me recently by a disillusioned friend. I told him that I believed there were still heroes among us, but that maybe we didn't always recognize them—that maybe we were confusing heroism with celebrity.

I have discovered one of those unrecognized heroes in the career of my friend, the late Jim Ingram, whose remarkable life story is appropriately entitled *The Hero Among Us: Memoirs of an FBI Witness Hunter*. Jim did not regard himself as a hero, but after his death and prior to the publication of this book, his editor, James L. Dickerson, insisted on adding the first phrase to the title. Jim rightfully deserves to be remembered as a hero for his service to his country over some 29 years as a special agent of the FBI.

That service included his involvement in investigating and helping solve some of the most infamous crimes of the late twentieth century. He was well-equipped to do that. Coming out of the harsh, demanding Great Depression years in the Oklahoma dust bowl, he knew about self-discipline and hard work. Those qualities served him well as he overcame difficult financial and family hardships to become a member of the FBI.

His career over the course of the next three decades would involve him in many a harrowing adventure. On his first assignment as a rookie agent in Indiana, he singlehandedly captured one of the most desperate criminals on the Top 10 Most Wanted List. For this he was singled out for commendation by FBI Director J. Edgar Hoover.

Not long after that he was assigned to New York City, arguably the most challenging of all the FBI offices outside Washington. Ingram was there when President Kennedy was assassinated in Dallas in November, 1963. For the next several months Jim would be engaged in the investigation of the background of Kennedy's assassin, Lee Harvey Oswald, and the role of his Cuban connection. Jim Ingram was believed to be one of the most knowledgeable of anyone in or out of the FBI on the details of that horrific crime. Despite all of the confusing speculation about it, he writes in this book that he believes that "Oswald was the lone gunman who acted on his own."

The next year saw Ingram being transferred at his request to Jackson, Mississippi where a new FBI office had been established to deal with the numerous civil rights crimes in the state, including the murder of three young men, two white and one black, in Neshoba County. This was a shameful and troubled time, and some local law enforcement authorities were either unable or unwilling to bring the perpetrators of those crimes to justice. Only the presence and persistence of the FBI ultimately broke the back of the Ku Klux Klan and its cowardly followers. Mississippi Governor Paul Johnson recognized the essential role which the FBI played in saving his state from the white racist fanatics. Ingram was the subject of every kind of threat imaginable. His book contains this chilling statement: "Had the FBI not challenged the Klan, we believe there would have been a total breakdown of law enforcement."

The six years of his assignment in Mississippi from 1964 to 1970 may have been the most dangerous period in the civil rights era. The Klan leadership started lashing out in all directions in its desperate effort to halt the forces of desegregation. The local representatives of the FBI were viewed as their most feared and visible foes. It was a period of terror marked by the burning of many black churches and the bombing of Jewish homes and places of worship, in addition to the assassination of civil rights leaders such as Medgar Evers and Vernon Dahmer in the state and ultimately Dr. Martin Luther King, Jr. in Memphis.

Ingram and his Mississippi-based FBI colleagues were in the forefront of the daunting task of ending the terror. Their lives were always on the line as they carried out their duties.

This involved the deadly process of infiltrating the ranks of the terrorists and bringing to justice the perpetrators of these horrible deeds. This difficult assignment frequently had to be carried out without the cooperation of local law enforcement officers some of whom were friendly with or intimidated by the Klan. Gradually the persistent work of the FBI coupled with the changes in the attitude of the public toward integration put an end to the terror.

But Jim Ingram's eventful career was by no means over. As he moved in the 1970's to the larger and more prestigious FBI offices in Washington, New York and Chicago, he found himself involved in solving many of the high profile cases that required the ultimate in resourcefulness and judgment. These included the sensational break-in of the offices of the Democratic National Committee at the Watergate in 1972.

At the same time there was a wave of violence in the cities against police officers, a bombing of a tavern that killed four people in the New York City financial district, and numerous other bombings across the country. Eleven were killed in a bombing at LaGuardia Airport during the Christmas holidays of 1975.

This volume includes gripping accounts of Ingram's involvement with training Special Forces for missions involving the Shah of Iran prior to and after his escape to the United States, the bizarre mass suicide and murder of over 900 people in the infamous Jim Jones nightmare in Guyana in 1978, and the details of some of the toughest law enforcement problems that the nation had ever faced.

Because of his reputation for courage and integrity, the Director of the FBI assigned him many of these most difficult cases. But finally the intensity of the work and some health issues caused Ingram, after 29 years of service to decide to retire. In January, 1982 he and his wife, Marie, came back to Mississippi to live out their lives in a less stressful setting in a place that they had come to love.

They were welcomed back and soon became actively involved in many community activities. After several years as vice-president for security at Mississippi's largest bank and after eight years as Commissioner of Public Safety of the State of Mississippi, Jim Ingram found an opportunity to perform what may now be looked upon as his greatest public service.

There were a number of "cold cases" from the 1960's involving murders by members of the Klan who were never brought to justice. Because of Ingram's familiarity with many of these cases, he was sought out to assist in bringing them back to life. Perhaps, the most notable one was that of the Neshoba County Klan member Edgar Ray Killen, who had never been convicted for his role in the murder of the three civil rights workers in Neshoba County in 1964.

This was right up Jim's alley. To the surprise and huge satisfaction of thousands of Mississippians his work with Attorney General Jim Hood and District Attorney Mark Duncan and a biracial citizen group known as the Philadelphia Coalition, resulted in Killen's conviction for which he received a sixty-year prison sentence.

That spectacular success was followed by another "cold case" prosecution of James Ford Seale, a Klansman who had avoided apprehension for two murders in 1964. Ingram provided some of the decisive testimony in that long-delayed trial that resulted in Seale's conviction.

Jim Ingram's life was devoted to serving his country, and this memoir is a reminder of the determination and courage that was required of him in carrying out his difficult and often thankless duties.

Former Mississippi Governor William F. Winter (1980-1984) was awarded the 2008 Profile in Courage Award by the John F. Kennedy Presidential Library and Museum. The William Winter Institute for Racial Reconciliation on the University of Mississippi's Oxford campus is named in his honor. He served as State Treasurer from 1964 to 1968, during the most violent years of the civil rights struggle in Mississippi.

"Jim Ingram made a big difference in Mississippi, and our folks will always appreciate him, his courage and his character. I was blessed to be his friend."

—Former Mississippi Governor Haley Barbour

"This is a simple story about a complex man who had a lasting effect on Mississippi. Jim Ingram was from the "old school" in the best sense of those words. He treasured traits like loyalty to others and loyalty to the law. He abhorred bullies and was fearless in tracking the "night riders" who used terror as their weapon of choice.

Question; who was the world famous Middle-Eastern dictator who took refuge in a "safe house" in Jackson, Mississippi…well, you'll just have to read the book and be stunned to find who was in our midst."

—Former Mississippi Secretary of State Dick Molpus

"Jim was always a big case guy—a long ball hitter. He didn't hit singles. He took the ball out of the park."

—Retired FBI Special Agent Bill Stokes

A young Jim Ingram saddled up and ready to ride

1

THE EARLY YEARS

Growing up in Oklahoma, I often stayed with my Grandpa Ingram out on the farm, where I sometimes slept three to a bed with my cousins. I learned a lot from my grandfather. He was a huge man, six foot four, and that was where I got my height. He had a limited education, but he read his Bible each night by kerosene lantern before he retired.

Grandpa taught me and my cousins the lessons of life. Some of those lessons were hard learned, such as the time we boys took it upon ourselves to take a melon from Grandpa Ingram's watermelon patch.

Not showing real good sense, we pirated it over beneath a tree and ate the heart out of the sweet melon. When Grandpa Ingram found out what we had done, he asked nonchalantly, speaking quietly, without showing any indication of the rage that he felt inside, if that was our watermelon?

Because of the easygoing tone of his voice, we thought it was just an ordinary question, nothing more.

"No, not really," we answered in unison.

"That's right—it's my watermelon," he answered, his voice rising somewhat. "Did you hoe the grass from around that watermelon patch?"

"No sir."

"I didn't think so."

In Grandpa's mind we had not done enough farm work to earn stealing a melon. Melons were a privilege, not a right.

"Now you have wasted a pretty good watermelon because the birds are now eating it," he continued. "Others could have enjoyed the cool taste of that watermelon."

"Yes sir."

"I'm going to have to teach you a lesson that you do not take something that is not yours."

"Yes sir."

By then we were getting pretty nervous.

Without explaining his intentions, he cut a large branch from a willow tree and proceeded, ever so slowly and deliberately, to cut the switch exactly the way he wanted it. In retrospect he probably took longer than needed—to draw out the suspense of the moment.

When he was done, he said sternly, "Jimmy (meaning me), you're first—bend over."

When he hit me with that switch, tears squirted from my eyes. I thought that was really hard but I endured it—and that was only the first lick. Many licks followed. He then treated each boy to the same number of licks.

Once the whacking was over, he said, "I hope I have taught each of you a lesson. You do not take something that is not yours, unless you get permission, and you do not waste God's fruit, which he has made to keep our bodies healthy."

We had two strikes against us.

I never forgot that lesson. In fact, I often recalled it when I thought about my huge grandpa. He was so respected by the other farmers and ranchers because he was such an honest person. When he dealt with others in the community, they always treated him with respect because he would show the same respect back to them. What I learned from that life lesson is that respect is contagious. It passes from person to person when the ground rules are followed.

My other grandfather, Grandpa Hall, also lived close by. Actually, I was named after that grandfather. I spent many an evening with him while he regaled me with stories that I truly enjoyed. My Grandpa Hall walked with a stooped shoulder because he had been shot at an early age by robbers and he still had one of the bullets in his back because doctors deemed it unsafe to remove. From that day on, he carried a .45-caliber pistol in his belt at all times. No one messed with my grandfather because they knew he would never endure another robbery or fight without retaliating.

My mother and father, Margaret and Walter Ingram, had arrived in Oklahoma in mule-drawn, covered wagons. They travelled separately and with their families, but they both settled in the little town of Henryetta, which is located in central Oklahoma. The town was founded on land belonging to the Creek Nation by a man named Hugh Henry, who was part Creek. He established a ranch and then discovered coal on his property, an event that attracted the attention of the St. Louis and San Francisco Railway, which brought whites to the area by the trainloads to mine the coal, maintaining a community of 5,000, about the size that it is today.

Henryetta is probably best known not for its coal, but for being the home of National Football League Hall of Fame quarterback Troy Aikman and Alice Ghostley, a Tony Award-winning actress recognized for her roles in *Bewitched, Designing Women, the Graduate*, and *To Kill a Mockingbird*. I didn't know her growing up, but we became close friends later in life when we both lived in New York City.

By the time I was born on January 22, 1932, Oklahoma and the rest of the country were in the early stages of the Great Depression. The national unemployment rate was around 20 percent. Banks were failing left and right. The year I was born the country was embroiled in a hotly contested presidential election, with President Herbert Hoover carrying the Republican banner, and Franklin D. Roosevelt representing the Democrats. Hoover argued that the government should stay out of the economy, while Roosevelt maintained government intervention was the only thing that would save the economy. Roosevelt won the election, of course, but not until America entered World War II did the country pull itself out of the Great Depression.

If you want to know what my childhood was like go back and reread John Steinbeck's *Grapes of Wrath,* the Noble Prize-winning novel about how the Great Depression and a relentless drought created the perfect storm for the Dust Bowl that sent desperate Oklahomans by the thousands to California to find work. The novel, which immortalized the places and events of my childhood, was set in Sallisaw, seventy miles from where I grew up. I am an "Okie" and proud of it.

My father was one of thirteen children, seven boys and six girls. I don't recall ever worrying about food, not even during the Depression, because my grandfather, Boston Ingram, had a farm just up the road from where we lived and he raised everything that the family needed to eat. He had a vegetable garden and he had cows, chickens, hogs, and goats. That was a good thing because it provided us with a security blanket while my father struggled during the Depression to make a living. We lived outside

Henryetta, near the highway. My father leased a service station and some tourist courts and cabins named Henryetta Modern Courts. Some of the units were stand alone, meaning they were not all hooked together like you see in motels. I watched my father struggle many times to make the lease payments. In those days, about the only people renting cabins were those fleeing the financial and environmental stresses associated with the Dust Bowl, and they didn't always have the money to pay.

* * *

Growing up in Henryetta was a lesson in history. I did not realize until I was actually in high school that there were no blacks attending any of the schools. There were a lot of Indians. Cherokee, Choctaw, Creeks. They were everywhere. The county in which we lived was the home of the Creek Nation. Despite their large numbers, you seldom saw Indian children in the public school system because they went to segregated Indian schools. The Indians were special to me because of the public activities, such as parades and other events, in which they participated.

In those days, the Indians did their snake dancing down Main Street with full headdress and costumes. It was a beautiful sight to behold. At that time Henryetta was known as a snake dancing town because snake dancing was legal. There was this one guy, a full blooded Indian, who dressed in his native garb and carried snakes with him in the parades. Sometimes he walked holding them, with some wrapped around his arms and his body. Other times he danced around them in the street as they slithered toward an unknown destination. Every once in a while the snakes would follow him as he marched up and down the street. It was the darnedest thing I'd ever seen. He was a pied piper of snakes. After I had grown up and left the area, they passed an ordinance and outlawed snake dancing.

I didn't realize it at the time, but we lived in a Jim Crow town. Most of the Indians were treated as second-class citizens and blacks were not allowed in town after 6 p.m. or sunset. Once there was a lynching of two black men accused of raping a white woman. As a result of the allegations, whites burned the black residential district and enacted a "sundowner" law that required blacks to leave town each day before sunset. Of course, the town was never able to live down its past. I got an early lesson on civil

20

rights and Jim Crow laws, but we, as young boys and girls, never thought much about it at the time.

*   *   *

I was nine when the Japanese bombed Pearl Harbor. All of my dad's brothers joined the military when World War II broke out, along with the uncles that my aunts married. The only reason my father did not join was due to ill health. My brother, Hubert, who was known as Hubo, enlisted in the Army Air Corps right out of high school. Much to our amazement he became a tail gunner on a B-29 bomber.

My job during those years was to take care of our cows, horses, goats, and hogs because my mother was busy and my brother was off at war. When the cows were ready to be bred it was my job to walk them about two miles to another farm, where I met the owner and helped him put them in the pen with the bull so he could take care of the cows. Afterward I would put the halter back on the cows and walk them back to our farm. Not only was I transportation director for the cows, I was witness to their amorous activities with the bull. When I returned home after a day of watching them do what animals do, Dad always asked, "Jimmy, did the bull take care of our cows?"

"I'd say, "Yes, Dad, he did."

"Well, did you watch it happen?"

"Yes, Dad, I did."

"So you know it happened?"

"Yes, Dad."

"Well, in that case I will pay the man for the bull."

In the early 1940s, my father started up the only bus line in Henryetta. He asked my Uncle Ray, who had been sent home from the war after being shot up in the chest and arms, to run the bus line. Basically, the bus line ran routes from downtown Henryetta to different parts of the county and back again. Because of the war there were no cars being manufactured. All the carmakers converted their factories to making airplanes and tanks. If you were lucky enough to already own a car you could not buy tires for it because they were all diverted to the war effort. Gasoline was rationed, as was meat. Tough times.

I was close to my Uncle Ray. One day, when we were playing football in my backyard, he rolled into me and I suffered a broken

21

leg below the knee. He always felt bad about that, but I didn't blame him. I was young and the leg healed. He and I always had a close bond.

Uncle Ray, being the handsome dude that he was, always attracted beautiful women when he drove the bus. The last bus of the day left downtown at 10 p.m. for the outlying areas. The first stop was always at the service station. When that happened people would get off to buy something or stretch their legs. I always noticed that there were two or three very attractive ladies sitting up front with Uncle Ray.

One day, he said, "Jimmy, I'm telling you there are so many love-starved women in this place. Sometimes I can't even get them off the bus."

Uncle Ray was a natural magnet for beautiful women.

I always remembered those women on the bus, about how they would go out on his run and then return with him. They just went along for the ride. When you're at war and everyone is tied up and the men are away, it is most difficult for the women. Later, Ray learned to play the steel guitar. Because he had a good voice, he started a band and performed in and around Henryetta. Then the women would hang onto him because he was a handsome guy who could sing. He always seemed to be in the right place at the right time.

I suppose my coming of age began with the bull and cows and then extended to the human population, starting with family. You learned a lot of things growing up in a family as large as mine. Although we lived in a pretty good-sized home with my grandpa, all the young kids slept in a bedroom next to Grandpa and Grandma. We learned a lot about how Grandma and Grandpa got thirteen children when the lights went out at night. We snickered and laughed, but not out loud because we knew that if Grandpa ever suspected that we knew what he was doing, that cane of his would come down over our heads with resounding force, so we muffled our laughter under our pillows and listened, our imaginations running wild.

By the time I was twelve, I had learned a great deal about the opposite sex. My older sister, Wanda, always had friends at the house and when they had dance parties they used me as the dummy dancer since I was the only male around. With all the men gone off to war, the only available male dancing talent was older men and high school kids.

I can well remember the dances they had on Saturday night. Before the night was over, the women without husbands would team up with what men were available and head to the woman's house. Once, while my aunt's husband was away in the military, four men walked her home from a dance. My dad saw this and he followed them and put a stop to their pursuit. My friend Jack and I watched the whole thing and I thought my dad was a very brave man because he took on four horny men, much younger, much bigger than he; but he asked them to leave my aunt alone and they did and I know she was happy for it. I never said anything to my dad about what I had witnessed. He never saw me lurking out in the dark that evening, watching. I always admired him after that because it took a strong man to do what he did.

* * *

During the war, I started delivering newspapers. My Grandpa bought me a horse for eleven dollars at auction and I rode that horse to deliver newspapers because I had a wide area to cover. It is amazing what you can see on a paper route, especially if it is an early morning paper route. You see people at their best, and at their worst. Front doors opened and closed at the crack of dawn. Back doors opened and closed. Car engines started and puttered down the road. Pretty soon you realized that secrets are the currency of many a marriage. You learn those things as a paperboy because they are enacted right in front of you.

My father was a Christian man, but knew that the courts and cabins were being used during the day by businessmen for illicit purposes and on the weekends by partygoers. That was just a way of life during that period. People did what they had to do to survive the war years. I recall one young man whose father was one of the premier businessmen in the Henryetta area. The father had some no-good sons and one of them ended up getting a teacher fired over a sex scandal. It was her first year at the school. She was a very attractive girl, but this guy, who already had graduated, ended up getting her in trouble and the school had to release her. This always sat in my craw because all he did afterward was brag about what he'd been able to do with this teacher. He was one of those who came to the courts late at night by cab with girls on his arm.

On two occasions, while the girls were asleep or taking a shower, he took their money and skipped, leaving them stranded.

One night, that guy came in a cab to pay for a room and he had a lady with him. I told him we were filled up. By that time, I had grown taller and filled out a little bit.

He said, "You can't be. I just called."

"I said, "We're filled up for you."

"Let me talk to that man there," he said, pointing to Grandpa.

He walked over and spoke to Grandpa, who said, 'Yeah, we've got a room."

I said, "No, we do not."

Grandpa said nothing.

The man said, "Look, you little shit—I know what you're trying to pull and I'm not going to put up with it."

"I don't like you," I said. "I've never liked you. I don't like anything about you."

"Well, I feel the same way about myself. There's lots of things I don't like about myself. But you've embarrassed me, and I'm not going to stand for it."

I said, "Well, do you want to be embarrassed a little further?"

"Why?"

"If you don't get in that cab and leave, I'm going to whip your ass right here. I've grown up a little bit. You're older, bigger, but you know what, I'm a hell of a lot meaner than you are and I know what you've done to these other women. You're a damn thief. I'm not going to have that anymore."

"I'm going to tell your father."

"Good."

"If I tell my father he is going to jump on your father."

"Good—then that's going to really give me a reason to jump your ass."

Backing down, he said, "I don't want any trouble."

"Well, you're going to have it. Get the hell out of here and don't come back."

He got in the cab and left. My grandpa smiled and said, "Jimmy, you've grown into a man."

"I don't know what I've grown into, but you are an honorable man. You've worked at this place. You've been shot and you carry a bullet where some crook shot you. You're my hero."

He smiled. "I really thought you would get whipped by that man."

"I probably would have. But he had more to lose than I did, Grandpa."

"Do you think you will have trouble with him in the future?"

"He knows I'm growing, getting stronger. He's not going to say anything to his daddy. Even if he does, my dad will only pat me on the back and say good work, son."

Later, I'd see that fellow around town and he'd make a point to walk across the street to keep from facing me. Knowledge is power. He had economic power. I had the kind of power that comes from knowing the truth. It was a standoff. One thing about being that age, the lessons kept coming, one after another, sometimes faster than I could keep up with them.

* * *

By the time I was fourteen, it was customary for everyone who worked at the service station and at the courts to pull 12-hour shifts. In the summer I worked from 6 p.m. to 6 a.m. My Grandpa always worried about me working at night because he was shot during a robbery at that same service station. Times were different back then. I always was very careful if a carload of men showed up. If they asked me to check their tires, and four or five of them went into the service station, it was like, "Sorry, you'll have to do that yourself." I had to do that because they could carry off half the store while I checked the tires.

My father always wanted me to work 6 to 6 because he said it would keep me out of trouble and he was right. Even when I got off at 6 a.m., I would dash home to milk the two cows and two goats, grab my horse and do my paper route. That way I was able to save a little money.

At the service station, I encountered a lot of old men who had no education whatsoever. During the war, the old men stayed in the mines, some of them getting deferments because the military needed the coal. I would sit out late at night and listen to these men. There would be a dozen men there telling old stories. I learned a lot from those men.

There was no television back then. Air-conditioning was unheard of. The old men enjoyed coming to the service station and telling old stories. During my football playing days, all those men came to Henryetta High School to watch me play ball, usually sitting together as a group. I was not the best ball player on the team, but they said, "Jim, you hustle, you're mean, and you play your heart out. That's all that we can ask of you." My football team had an unusual name. At first, they called the team the Mud Hens. Then the name was shortened to simply Hens. Thinking that was too bland, they changed it to the Fighting Hens, a truly bizarre name for a football team if you think about it.

In a nearby community, there was a honky-tonk called the Linger Longer. It stayed open all night. The owner was a very decent individual, an immigrant. He did business at the station and was a good friend of my father's. On Saturday nights they always had live music and almost three-quarters of the people there were females since the men were all off at war. The women would dance with women, older men too old to fight in the war, or high school boys too young to serve in the military.

Sometimes sailors on leave showed up at the dances. Whenever that happened there were always four or five women after each sailor. They must have thought that the women in our little town were all loved-starved. It was always interesting after the dances because the men, with three or four women in tow, would head to the courts to party. The single courts rented for $2.50 a night. A double with two beds was five dollars a night. A real bargain for not-so-true love.

By the time I was thirteen I helped Grandpa each morning when he cleaned the rooms. Many times I went with him to pull the sheets off the beds and all that. I saw many things because the motel was also used by business people from other communities who would drive up with their girlfriends and use the cabin for an hour and then leave. Some men stayed longer than others. I always got involved because Grandpa would say, "Jimmy, number six cabin needs some ice."

I'd get some ice from the service station and take it to the cabin. Usually the door would never swing all the way open and I wouldn't see who was inside. The person would grab the ice and hand me a quarter or a dime or sometimes nothing at all.

Service station and Henryetta Modern Courts

I cannot even guess how many women were left at the cabins at night after parties by the men who used them for sex and then slipped out and drove away, leaving them stranded. When that happened, Grandpa would call me early the next morning and say, "Jimmy, you need to go to room so and so with me. There is a woman there, stranded, and we've got to ask her to leave."

Many times the women would be crying, upset that they had shacked up with a guy who'd stranded them. Many occasions we would have those individuals take money from the women's pocket books and leave them without enough money to get home. I've seen Grandpa take money from his pocket and say, "Where do you need to go? I'll pay for it." Grandpa was always good about that. Many times he would say, "Jimmy, you stay here and make sure the cabbie gets to the right cabin and she is taken care of."

I saw those ladies every now and then on the streets of Henryetta. Some would smile. Others would look away, embarrassed. My junior year, I ran into one of the women I'd helped and I smiled at her. She smiled back. Then she stopped me and said, "My husband and I went to a Henryetta football game the other day and watched you play. You have grown into a stud."

"Well I don't know about that."

"You lost the game but I watched you on every play. You are a heck of a football player."

Changing the conversation, I said, "I hope you are happy."

"I'm very happy," she said, smiling one last time before walking away.

*   *   *

After the crowd left the Linger Longer, everyone would stop at the service station because we had a line of groceries. We had one group of Henryetta businessmen and their wives who would stop and buy different things—eggs, meat, bread—and they'd take the food and go home to prepare breakfast for the group. Usually they were steeped in liquor because they had been drinking all night.

One morning I was asked to cut some ham for them to take with them. I washed my hands and started cutting the ham. One of the ladies, who I always thought was a very nice person, asked, "What's your name?"

"Jimmy."

"Well, Jimmy I bet that's the first ham you ever cut. Give me all you can give me."

Everyone laughed, enjoying the ribald joke at my expense.

After a little while, she said, "Why don't you let me do that? I can tell you've never cut any meat in your life."

She started laughing and everyone laughed.

One old boy said, "Jimmy, you've never had any have you?"

I said, "No sir, I haven't."

They all had a good laugh over that at my expense.

A couple of years later, when I was seventeen, we were dancing at the town hall and I was with this girl. I was dancing away when I saw her parents and I walked her back to them. It was the same woman who had made fun of me being a virgin. She looked at me sternly, seeing her daughter's hand in mine.

I said something I immediately regretted. She looked at me and I thought, *that was nasty of me*. Later that evening, I walked back over to her and apologized. "I couldn't resist what I said. You've got the sweetest daughter."

"Thank you," she said.

The man sitting next to her did not say a word.

It was just something I had to do. I was not a mean-spirited person. I know one thing. That lady remembered well what she

28

said at my expense. It was one of those things that stick with you while you're growing up. No one likes to be laughed at, especially if there is degrading innuendo attached to the laughter.

* * *

Later Dad sold all his interest in the cabins and the service station and became the postmaster, a position he got because he had become very friendly with U.S. Senator Robert Kerr and our Congressman Bill Stigler. He had these people for dinner at our house on many occasions. It paid off. They made him the postmaster. We were all glad to get rid of the tourist courts.

Once Dad sold his interest in the courts and moved uptown, so to speak, that gave me the opportunity to concentrate on high school, football, and basketball. I was an average student, but I enjoyed school. Every morning I hitchhiked to Henryetta High School. We traveled that way because few people owned cars. At night I hitchhiked back home. It was very simple to do because most of the people would know you. During this period, our coach, Marion Anglin, had been at the high school for years. He was inducted into the High School Coaches Hall of Fame. He was always very nice to me. He felt I had potential and he wanted to work on that potential. At that time, Henryetta had no sports for females. Sports were a males-only pursuit.

My basketball team ended up going to the state finals my senior year and we were beaten by a very good Oklahoma City team. Our football team was lousy. I think we won three and lost ten. I wanted to go to college and my mother and father wanted me to be the first in the family to go to college, but they could not afford to send me. I had saved some money from working at the service station and the courts, but not nearly enough. Dad advised me to select a school and then find a way to pay my way.

It was during this time that I became very fond of one of my schoolmates, Marie Howard. She and I had speech class together. She came from a very nice, hard working family in Henryetta. We were both sixteen when we started dating and were very much in love. She was a beautiful girl with an outgoing personality. Her parents, Tom and Elsie Howard, ran a small restaurant on Main Street. On occasion black people would come around to the side door and Babe Howard, Marie's mother, would allow them to come into the kitchen where she had a table and chair set up.

29

Defying local tradition, she fed those who were hungry. Soon it became known to people passing through Henryetta. A state highway that lead to the capital in Oklahoma City ran straight through Henryetta and many blacks passed the word that if you were hungry and wanted to get something to eat in a restaurant, all you had to do was knock on the side door of Babe Howard's kitchen and you would be welcomed and fed with respect.

I never observed any racial problems in Henryetta, except on one occasion, when I was playing with a friend at their farm. My friend's father came into the barn where we were playing, and yelled at an older black man that he was not doing what he was supposed to do in the barn. He called him the "n" word and my friend, as well as me, felt badly about his treatment.

As young kids sometimes do, after graduation Marie and I got married in August without the approval of our parents. My father was furious, as well as Marie's family. But we did it and we could not explain why. It was a spur of the moment thing. Our plan was to leave Henryetta and seek our fortune in college. That thought didn't last long because neither of us had any funding whatsoever.

One day late in August I was walking down Main Street in Henryetta and looked up and there was Coach Anglin with a huge man, about six foot seven and weighing about 300 pounds. He said, "Jimmy, come here. We've been looking for you. This is Coach Red Robinson, Northeastern Oklahoma A&M, and he wants to give you a try."

I stuttered and stammered. The big coach said, "Yes, Ingram, I have two scholarships left. Coach tells me that you're a hitter and you're mean enough to make my ball club."

I said, "Coach . . . ," and my words frittered out into nothing.

I was totally at a loss for what to say.

He said, "Be in Miami, Oklahoma at such and such date. We're starting tryouts. If you can make it, you've got yourself a scholarship. If you can't, then it's up to you whether you want to enroll in school. We are going to have a two-day tryout and we'll see if you are a ballplayer. I've also agreed to take Garland Ward, the quarterback, because the coach tells me he's just about the only other player who might could make it."

Jim Ingram at Northeastern Oklahoma A&M

"Coach I'll be there."

I could not wait to tell Marie and my parents.

When the time came to leave Henryetta, Garland Ward's parents took us about 200 miles away to Miami, Oklahoma, right on the Missouri-Kansas-Oklahoma border. It was a very nice city, a good sized school. The first day I walked out on the field, I met fifteen University of Florida players. I didn't realize that Red Robinson had an agreement to take University of Florida players. They were freshmen, not good enough to make the traveling squad at Florida. Once I looked them over, I thought, *Oh, my God, I'll never make it*. I figured I would have a tough time.

I hit, bit, scratched, and did everything possible to make that ball club. The player from Florida I had to beat to win the position was bigger than I was, so I had no choice but to go all out if I wanted to get a scholarship. Without a scholarship, I knew I would return to Henryetta and probably never get a college education.

One afternoon, after a hard workout, Coach Robinson came up to me and said, "Ingram, I've got you a scholarship. You're my defensive end. That boy from Florida can play the other end. You're exactly what I'm looking for. I understand you're married."

"Yes sir."

"We've got some apartments that were built during World War II and they're in good shape. I've picked you out the best one. Bring your wife on. We're going to get her a job at school."

"Thank you, thank you, thank you."

I couldn't believe my good fortune.

During the first two weeks I roomed with some outstanding men who later helped me considerably. One of them, Bill Pace, subsequently became head football coach at Vanderbilt University.

Another roommate, Bennie Lee, went on to become a coach at the University of Kansas. Outstanding ball players, both of them, and very good friends of baseball legend Mickey Mantle, with whom they had played semi-pro baseball. At that time, Mickey was playing shortstop with a Class D minor league team, the Independence (Missouri) Yankees, a farm team owned by the New York Yankees.

**Jim and Marie Ingram with their three sons
—Jim, center, and Steve and Stan**

During the first two weeks of training, Mickey came over to the apartments where we lived and visited Bennie and Bill. I got to know him well during those visits. He was just a good old country boy. At the time, I had no idea of the greatness of Mickey Mantle.

The next year they called him up from Kansas City to the Yankees. Bill and Bennie always kept in touch with him, and he did come to see a couple of our ball games.

Garland Ward, who went with me to A&M, was released after two days, replaced by a quarterback from University of Florida. Garland told me, "Jimmy I'm leaving. I'm not going to be able to make it. I'm going to enroll at the University of Oklahoma." He did and enjoyed a great career there.

In October 1951, Northeastern A&M students elected a 29-year-old World War II veteran, William Bennett, as their student council president. I was asked to introduce him to the assembly. Explaining that he was not the type of person who liked to talk about his personal life, I pointed out that he had killed 57 enemy soldiers while serving in Germany and had been awarded the Purple Heart with three clusters for being wounded four times and had received the Distinguished Service Cross. I concluded by

33

pointing out that he had fought heroically, not only for his own life, but for the American way of life.

This was my first public speaking challenge and it prepared me for what was to come in my career as an FBI agent. Later in my career, I discovered that I was reaching for a microphone much more frequently than for my firearm.

While in college, Marie and I were blessed with the birth of twin sons, Steve and Stan, born in 1951, the arrival of which started us out on the adventure of a lifetime.

Miami, Oklahoma was just the beginning.

2

THEY DON'T TEACH YOU
ABOUT NAKED MADAMS
AT THE FBI ACADEMY

After two years at Northeastern Oklahoma A&M, I received an athletic scholarship from George Washington University to play football. Marie and I and our two sons packed up and left Oklahoma for the first time in our lives. We drove halfway across the country to Washington, D.C., which might as well have been a foreign country, at least culturally.

Oklahoma Senator Robert "Bob" Kerr, whose family owned the Kerr-McGee Oil Company, offered me a job as a doorman and elevator operator at the U.S. Senate Building, where I had the opportunity on a daily basis to meet senators and representatives and other government officials. I like to consider myself a people person. That's why I enjoyed meeting so many people while doing that work. My job was to open the doors when I saw someone start into the building, or, when I was assigned to the elevator, holding the door open while people entered and exited the elevator, followed by the inevitable, "What floor please?"

They were not positions that you needed a lot of intellect to handle, so you ended up using your personality to make the position more interesting. My goodness, so many people were kind enough to ask, "What's your name?" Part of my job was to know all the senators' names. Being the doorman to the U.S. Senate Building can be a very high-profile position. Certainly, it led to better things for me.

In January 1953 I observed the inauguration of Dwight D. Eisenhower. He had soared from World War II hero to president. As I stared out the window, about as close as you could be to the inaugural ceremony without holding the Bible, I noticed that there were no black faces anywhere to be seen. I think the only females I recall in the crowd with the president were Mamie Eisenhower and Pat Nixon. That was about it. The America that I saw in the 1950s was light years away from what it is today. What a journey that has been!

One of the elected officials I met was Congressman Ed Edmundson from Oklahoma, who remarked during one of our many conversations, "Ingram, when you decide what you want to do in life, come see me."

Eventually, I took him up on his offer. His background was in law enforcement as a former attorney general and former FBI agent. He wanted to know if I would be interested in a position with the FBI. He told me I wasn't old enough to be an FBI agent, because at that time you had to be twenty-five years of age or older, but he volunteered to make some telephone calls to see what he could do to get me on board at some level.

"Thank you very much, sir."

I came to my feet, ready to leave.

"Sit down, Ingram," he said, smiling. "I'm going to make the calls right now. I know some people at FBI headquarters."

With me sitting there, he set up some appointments for me. Never in my born days did I ever dream about being an FBI agent, traveling the world. Congressman Edmundson put all that in motion for me simply by making a few telephone calls on my behalf. Not only did he have clout as a congressman, he had influence as a former FBI agent. I can't imagine anyone in my position having a better employment reference.

On June 25, 1953, FBI Director J. Edgar Hoover sent a directive to the Oklahoma City bureau to initiate an investigation into my "character, reputation, ability and qualifications" for the position of clerk in the fingerprint office of the FBI. Ordering that the Civil Service Commission and the House Committee on Un-American Activities be checked for information about me, Hoover wrote: "I desire that you cause a very complete and thorough investigation to be made of this applicant. The inquiries made should not be confined to the references given (by the applicant), as experience shows they are usually favorable. Anything that your investigation may disclose further than the above references should be reported." After conducting numerous interviews, the agent who headed up the investigation concluded: "(Ingram) is a very good prospect for future agent material . . . is alert, keen and tactful."

I ended up being hired by the FBI in August 1953 as a clerk in the fingerprint identification division, the idea being that I could apply to be an agent once I turned twenty-five. To our relief, Marie also was given a job with the FBI. In the blink of an eye we both became part of the most powerful *government* in the world. Imagine that. Even as I worked in the fingerprint division at the FBI, I remained a student at George Washington University, where I majored in history and worked to complete my pre-law coursework so that I could attend law school. I was scheduled to get my bachelor's degree in June 1954.

After only five months on the job, I realized I could only burn so many candles at both ends. I was a fulltime student and FBI employee. Marie also worked fulltime. It was during this time that our twin sons, Steve and Stan, developed severe asthma. It was difficult enough to arrange child care for them, but when you added frequent illnesses and doctor's visits into that mix it became clear that something had to change. If Marie quit her job to stay at home with our sons, we would not have enough income to survive. The only solution was to ask the FBI to transfer me to Oklahoma, where we could obtain help from our parents with the children.

On February 2, 1954, I met with my supervisor, G. J. Engert, to discuss my increasingly desperate situation. He was very sympathetic and on that same day sent a memo to his supervisor explaining my situation. "Due to the health of his twin sons he is in question as to whether he is going to have to leave the Bureau," he wrote in the memo. "His two boys have asthma and have been under the care of Dr. Sorking. He believes this climate has a greater affect on the boys' condition and that possibly the climate in Oklahoma would be more suitable . . . He and his wife have used practically all of their leave in order to stay at home and take care of the children when they are ill. He is very reluctant to leave the Bureau . . . If at all possible he would like to get a transfer to Oklahoma City where he could be at home where his parents could help take care of the children. He would also be able to finish his education, either at the University of Oklahoma at Norman, or at Oklahoma City University. Ingram would accept a transfer at any grade in order to return home. This employee presents an excellent appearance and has an excellent attitude toward his work and the

Bureau. I believe he would be a definite asset to the Bureau in any assignment given him."

Nine days later the Oklahoma City office sent Director Hoover a memorandum that explained that there were no clerical vacancies in the office. Concluded the memo: "Consequently it will not be possible to transfer either Mr. or Mrs. Ingram to Oklahoma City."

What a disappointment that was. We were both almost out of leave. I loved the FBI. I loved the idea of becoming an agent with the Bureau. But as much as I wanted a career with the FBI, my family came first. After thinking about it for two weeks, I submitted my resignation to Mr. Hoover. "I am reluctant to leave the bureau because I have enjoyed working here and have made many new friends, but I find that I must leave, because of the health of our two children. I would have liked to have stayed with the Bureau, as I have ambitions to become an FBI agent; I surely appreciated working for the bureau."

Within ten days I received a letter from Mr. Hoover himself, accepting my resignation. He concluded by asking for a forwarding address and stating, "It is a pleasure to know you have enjoyed your work with the Bureau and I am indeed sorry to learn that the health of your twin sons has made the submission of your resignation necessary."

We left Washington, D.C. in March 1954, convinced that my career with the FBI was at an end. First we went to Henryetta, where we spent some time with our families before setting out to Oklahoma City, where I enrolled at Oklahoma City University. We were close enough to our families to get help with the children when we needed it, but far enough away to begin a new life.

I found work and focused on completing my education as a part-time student at Oklahoma City University. Whether it was the change in climate—or simply because our sons outgrew their asthma attacks—their health improved to the point where those issues were no longer a consideration. While still attending Oklahoma City University, I applied for a position at the Oklahoma City FBI office as a security guard, beginning work on May 30, 1956. I have never felt any work was beneath me. It's how you do the job that counts. Not so much the job itself.

Although I was only filling in for the regularly assigned security guard, I was happy to get the work—and enthused to again be on the FBI payroll. I had travelled to Washington with dreams of becoming a professional football player. When that dream dimmed, I succumbed to the dream of becoming an FBI agent. In 1956, when the fulltime security guard at the Oklahoma City office was accepted for FBI agent training, I was given his position, along with an increase in salary.

During this time, Marie and I were graced with the birth on November 24, 1956, of our third son, James. Within weeks I received my first letter since my resignation from Director Hoover, who wrote: "I would like to take this opportunity to offer Mrs. Ingram and you my congratulations on the birth of your son, James. It is my sincere wish that your little boy's future will be filled with good health and happiness."

Was I back in the loop? How often do regular Joe's receive congratulatory letters from J. Edgar Hoover? I was optimistic that I still had a chance with the FBI. Scheduled to receive my B.A. degree from Oklahoma City University in May 1957, I applied for Special Agent training after I saw a radiogram captioned "SA Applicants—New Agents Class Scheduled for June 17, 1957."

In April, I filled out an application. I was sent to Tinker Air Force Base in Oklahoma City to receive a physical examination. During my interview, I was questioned about my previous resignation due to the health of our twins. I explained that they were two years of age when they were experiencing asthma problems, but they were five now and had had their tonsils and adenoids removed and were in excellent health.

Then I was asked the most crucial question of my career.

"Are there factors of any kind, health of family or otherwise that will limit your availability for assignment in any office where your services are needed?"

"No sir," I answered.

It was the answer they wanted to hear.

On May 10, 1957, I was offered a probationary appointment as a Special Agent at the unheard of salary of $5,915 a year. The appointment was for one year during which time I would have to complete training at the academy. I was ordered to report to the Washington, D.C. office on June 17. When I first went down that path, I knew that if I was not prepared I would not make it. They let you know the first day you arrive what is expected of you. If you do not measure up, you will be gone immediately. You would be tested almost daily, not only academically and physically, but you had to withstand the rigors of training as you went from day to day. If they thought there was better material elsewhere they would inform you and you would be gone. Period. If you did not hustle. If you did not work. If you did not make required academic scores— and you were tested every day—then they'd show you the door. They were not going to give you anything. You had to earn it.

You had to stay up late at night and prepare yourself for each day, because it was seven days a week. The only time you had off was Sunday morning to attend church and do your laundry. You must always be available. You had day classes, night classes. There was no spare time whatsoever and that was good. Many men were single, but there were those of us who were married. We had three sons by that time. During this period, Marie spent time with her parents, waiting for me to graduate and get an assignment. You can see how critical that was in the event I did not make the grade and was sent packing back to where I came from.

The FBI Academy was on the grounds of the Quantico Marine Corps base in rural Virginia, located about 35 miles southwest of the nation's capital. The first classroom at the campus was built in 1940 and it was fairly sparse, but by the time I arrived on campus on June 17, 1957, a new wing and additional dining space had been added. The firing range could be reached only by experiencing a noisy, bumpy bus ride. The facility was replaced in 1972 by a modernized 547-acre campus that featured a new firing range, two seven-story dormitories, and a 1,000-seat auditorium. It was quite an upgrade to the facility I attended. When I was there as a trainee we slept eight to a room and attended cramped classrooms. There was no way to ever have a moment's privacy.

I remember the day I arrived on campus quite well. Reporting to Quantico and meeting over fifty men who had arrived for the same FBI agents' class was an eye-opening experience. Number one, I noted there were no females, no blacks, no American Indians, no Asians—just fifty white men from all across the United States. I realized I had my work cut out for me because this was a very difficult three-month training course. In fact, within a matter of two days, I looked around and there were already three people gone. A week later, four others left. I learned to keep my mouth shut and not ask too many questions on why they left the training program. Some left of their own accord. Some were asked to leave. The training courses continued seven days a week. It was very exhausting, but it was an experience I never dreamed I would ever have.

In the dining room, you went to a certain table and you sat down. There was no cafeteria. You had a certain amount of food to a table. Everyone made sure that they took sufficient food. The main thing was that they had a seat for you. You would go to class the next morning and maybe the seat next to you would be empty. That meant that during the night they took the guy's notebook and sent him packing. You didn't ask questions. You might have eight or nine people who didn't make it. The first you knew about it was you would see the empty chair. In a few minutes, they'd say, "Let's tighten up the class. Let's move up one."

You knew that guy wouldn't be coming back. You just didn't ask about him. The instructors, or Counsel as they called them, were also under the gun. They were under more stress than we were. They had to look good also. If someone wasn't doing his homework, it made them look bad as instructors.

Sometimes football players are called and they're told, "Bring your playbook, you're finished." That was the way it was with us. If they asked for your notebook, you knew that you were a goner. If you had an old boy for a friend and he stumped his toe and he messed up in your presence, you could see he wouldn't make it. I want to make it clear that making it through the training was not an easy thing to do.

At this time, the FBI was under the leadership of Director J. Edgar Hoover, who as we all know, was criticized on a regular basis by the public and the media, but I learned to love the man, as not only my director, but because I always felt that if you are going to work for an organization, or a person, either be loyal or get out. And I was loyal. As we proceeded through the training, I enjoyed the benefits of making lasting friendships. For years afterward, I conversed telephonically with individuals that I was in training with. One agent in particular talked weekly with me about the old days, especially about our friendships within the bureau.

41

*   *   *

While I was at the training academy, I learned all aspects of law enforcement. But at the same time I was taught how to deal with all types of people during interviews, as well as what to expect generally as an FBI agent. In the 1950s the FBI was certainly ahead of the curve as far as the Miranda rights were concerned, so we had a lot of legal training outside the types of training you would expect, such as firearms instruction. At the beginning of that training I was very nervous and had considerable difficulty meeting minimum requirements.

I was a disgrace as an Oklahoma boy because I just couldn't shoot worth a damn. I was wearing glasses at the time for nearsightedness. My instructors and I discussed it and we concluded that I shot a lot better without my glasses. According to the firearms instructor's report: "His ability improved to a marked degree [without glasses]. It is believed that with additional training and experience, he will gain self-confidence and his firearms ability will continue to improve. Firearms qualifications certified."

During the training, I fired the .38-caliber revolver, .45-caliber Thompson submachine gun, 12-gauge shotgun, .30-caliber rifle, and the Federal gas gun. Later, I learned that during this training period and subsequent training in 1965, 1973, and 1981, I fired approximately 1,440 rounds of ammunition of various calibers.

So what if I wasn't the best shot in the FBI? That just meant that I had to improve my skills at talking my way out of difficult situations. It is a skill I worked on my entire life.

When it came time for the remaining group, which by now had dwindled to half its original size, to graduate, we were told we would have to meet Mr. Hoover. We were instructed on what to do and what not to do. When you meet Mr. Hoover, you let him do the talking and then you move on. He always had a gathering for the graduating class at the Mayflower Hotel.

It was a humbling experience for many of the old country boys, but you had to look your sharpest. Mr. Hoover evidently agreed that each individual in my group passed his muster, so to speak, and we were each given our orders. Mine happened to be Indianapolis, Indiana. Today Indianapolis is probably best known as the home of a top-ranked football team, but in those days the

To James O. Ingram
Best wishes
6.11.07   J. Edgar Hoover

43

city's most enduring claim to fame was as the home of the Ku Klux Klan. I wasn't sure what to expect when I arrived.

* * *

At the time of my first assignment, Marie and I did not have sufficient funds to immediately transport the entire family to our new home, so I went ahead of them and lived in a flop house for a few weeks until I had enough money saved to bring my family.

My first introduction to Indianapolis was to be welcomed by thieves. One morning I walked out of the apartment and saw that my Ford automobile was down on all four rims. Someone had stolen all four tires. There was an article in the *Indianapolis Star* along with a photograph of my car. The headline read: "Welcome G-man." Thought I'd never live that down.

Not long after that I met G. Gordon Liddy, who also was assigned to the Indianapolis office. He was a most unusual individual and there was no doubt in anyone's mind that he was a very well-trained, intelligent agent who came from a good background. He had a beautiful wife who was a school teacher. Everyone enjoyed being around Liddy. We called him two-gun Liddy because he usually carried two weapons on his person at all times.

In later years Liddy gained a reputation as a tough guy, but that wasn't the case when he first arrived in Indianapolis. On his first day, Liddy strolled into the Indianapolis FBI office to report for duty wearing an impeccable, three-piece, charcoal gray Rogers-Peet suit that he had purchased in New York, looking every bit the citified dandy.

The Special Agent in Charge obviously had a sense of humor. For his first assignment, Liddy was instructed to participate in a surveillance operation at a funeral home for the purpose of apprehending a wanted fugitive who was expected to attend services for his deceased wife. He was told to wear his fancy suit and pose as a casket salesman while a second agent hid in the closet with a two-way radio. In those days, the only place you would see a suit like Liddy's was at a funeral home. He had no idea he was being type cast.

Liddy took part in the funeral and the burial, working as an undertaker's assistant, but the fugitive never showed up. Later,

44

Liddy wrote in his autobiography: "I put the Rogers-Peet suit into mothballs and bought more appropriate clothing."

*   *   *

In Indianapolis it was easy to make friends with the old timers because they were always eager to take in a new, green agent and embarrass him as much as possible. One day, not long after I arrived, one of the agents asked me to go with him to cover an investigation. We went to a shady part of town. He knocked on the door of a nondescript house in an unremarkable neighborhood.

I heard a woman's voice say, "Come in."

We opened the door and walked it. We were greeted by a fully clothed woman who said, "Hold on, let me get the misses for you."

The agent said, "Jimmy, have a seat."

I sat, not sure what to expect.

All of a sudden in comes a naked woman that I was soon to learn was a madam in a house of prostitution. She was not a small lady by any means. She had coal-black hair and a solid white body. No sun had ever touched her face, legs, and body. I'm sitting there with my mouth wide open, and the agent turns to me and asks, "Why are you staring?"

My eyes immediately dropped to the floor as the woman, who was probably in her mid-50s, sat on the sofa. She had a few pounds on her, but with her it looked good. All the agent wanted to do was stare at me. No one said a word for what seemed like an eternity; then the agent started laughing. Grinning broadly, the woman got up and left the room, returning moments later wearing a gown. Then the two of them laughed together.

Finally, she said, "Welcome to Indianapolis!"

The madam was one of the agent's informants. The visit was all a setup to see how a greenhorn would react. I reacted like all the others before me, not knowing what to do next. I always remember that so well because when I returned to the office with that old-time agent there was a gallery of agents waiting for us to arrive.

"Well, Ingram, did you have a good day?" they asked, laughing.

I knew I had been set up, but it was enjoyable because you knew that if they did not like you they would not have accepted you into their little group. The madam was a trusted source of the agent who introduced me to her. You have a source and you have a backup connected with the source or informant. You seldom have

45

one where you have only one person connected. In this case, the madam collected information from the girls and passed it on to the agent.

Agents usually have a madam in their reservoir of sources. The agent in charge of the office will always know the identity of the informant. It may be like in Indianapolis or Jackson, Mississippi, where the informants number (JN423, for example) is buried in the file on the background they do on an individual. The supervisor should know the identity of the informant, along with the designated agent and the backup agent. When someone is transferred, the agent will tell the informant something like, "I am leaving, but John will be your contact." Most times the informant will accept that and continue to provide information.

* * *

Eventually I was assigned to work the Federal Correctional Complex in Terre Haute, a city of about 60,000 residents. The complex has a medium security facility and one that houses inmates serving federal death sentences. My partner was Leo Ford, a Native American from Colorado. What a delight it was to be around Leo. He taught me many things about dealing with prison inmates, the main thing being you'd better be on your best game. It took me a long time to learn the tricks of the trade on how to conduct interviews with them. There were seasoned Mafia prisoners, seasoned bank robbers, seasoned killers, all of them serving time there for various reasons. There was a large contingent of people from Chicago, who had their own way of doing things. For me, it was a case of learn or perish. I wasn't going to educate them on my ways of doing things. I had to learn theirs if I wanted to survive.

My first real challenge involved an Oklahoma outlaw named Ben Golden McCollum, who had escaped from an Oklahoma prison in 1954 after serving more than two decades of a 40-year sentence. He was immediately put on the FBI 10 Most Wanted Fugitives list. Back in the 1920s, McCollum was nicknamed the "Sheik of Boynton." He robbed banks all across Oklahoma, garnering a reputation as a Jesse James-style outlaw who robbed from the rich to the delight of the poor, but he was captured in 1929 while walking the streets of Boynton, Oklahoma. He was convicted, and sent to prison.

By the time I arrived in Indiana, McCollum had eluded capture for about four years. As luck would have it, I was able to track him to an Indianapolis boarding house, where I took him into custody without incident on an unlawful flight to avoid confinement and murder warrant. For a rookie agent, capturing a Top 10 Wanted List criminal was a big deal. Within days I received a letter from Director Hoover: "You demonstrated admirable resourcefulness and aggressiveness in discharging your assignment, thereby contributing to the success attained. This was a job very well done." Despite my efforts, McCollum was paroled three years later. He relocated to Kentucky and was shot to death by two youthful robbers who had no idea who he was. It was just a matter of bad luck on McCollum's part.

I can see how inquiring minds would wonder how the McCollum arrest came about. Did we capture him because of a tip from someone in the boarding house? Did someone in prison get word of his location and pass the information along to us? Or did someone from back home in Oklahoma, perhaps a distant cousin, get word to me by way of the grapevine? I'd love to tell you, but informants are the backbone of witness hunting. Like a good newspaper reporter, I never reveal my sources.

On a day-to-day basis, we received leads from all over the country to interview certain inmates about their knowledge of a certain crime. Those were busy days, but ones I will always cherish because I will always remember how I would spend all day interviewing some of the toughest individuals in the prison system. Doing that you learn the tools of the trade—eye contact, body language, how they react to certain questions. At the same time you knew that some days they had you and some days you had them. Many an inmate I would work until I finally got what I wanted from that individual. Incidentally, this is the same federal prison where Timothy McVeigh was executed for his part in the Oklahoma City bombing.

This was a very, very tough penitentiary. Many of the individuals were sent there because they were incorrigible, mean individuals who would kill you in a moment. In addition to interviewing inmates for the purpose of obtaining information about crimes under active investigation, we also had to handle cases involving assaults on other inmates and penitentiary officials.

This assignment was the one that started me on the road to learning the skills necessary to conduct interviews and how to break an individual down, because those are the tools of the trade. You learned you had to treat some individuals differently than others. Those years were very good for me and prepared me for my next assignment: New York City.

In his report on my October 1959 transfer, the assistant director of the administrative division wrote: "Ingram has participated in raids and dangerous assignments, and his performance has been highly satisfactory. As a resident agent at Terre Haute, he has received excellent training and experience in the handling of criminal type violations." He went on to point out that the *Terre Haute Tribune-Star* recently had published an editorial titled "A Salute to the FBI."

The favorable reference to the FBI, he explained, was a tribute to the Bureau and the personnel assigned to the Terre Haute office. The editorial read, in part: "Proud of their profession, local agents maintain a standard of conduct and action that demands respect. FBI men must meet a high moral, education and physical standard. By insisting on this type of man, the spirit, of the FBI is molded. Terre Haute is indeed fortunate in having these outstanding citizens and patriots in our community."

The inferences for my future were clear.

New York would have its hands full topping my Indiana experiences.

Indianapolis FBI agents and wives at Christmas party.
G. Gordon Liddy, left, at the far end of the table,
with Jim Ingram and Marie, right front

3

ASSASSINATION OF A PRESIDENT

It was November 22, 1963.

"The president has been shot! The president has been shot!"

I heard the words as soon as I stepped out onto a Manhattan street from a subway exit. At first I thought it was some kind of a cruel joke. Then I considered the possibility that the man shouting the words might be deranged, all the more so since he was darting in and out of traffic without any regard for his own safety. I hadn't been living in New York City long, but I'd been there long enough to expect the unexpected on the city streets.

Within seconds the man was gone, the urgency of his words dissipating into the ordinary sounds of the city—car horns, disjointed conversations, the roar of construction machinery. With my heart pounding, I rushed to the FBI office, where I knew I would find out the truth.

Two hundred miles away, FBI Director J. Edgar Hoover placed an urgent telephone call from his Washington office. U.S. Attorney General Robert Kennedy was pulled away from a late lunch at a daylong conference on organized crime to take the call.

"I have news for you," said Hoover, forgoing a traditional greeting.

"What?" asked Kennedy.

"The president has been shot."

Hoover's voice was cold, matter of fact. Brutal some would say. He paused to allow his words to sink in. There was no love lost between Hoover and Robert Kennedy. After a long moment of silence, Robert Kennedy said, "What? Oh. I—is it serious? I –." Clearly, he was in shock.

"I think it's serious," continued Hoover. "I am endeavoring to get details. I'll call you back when I find out more." Forty-five minutes later he called back. Again, his words were blunt, with no conversational buildup to lessen the pain: "The president's dead."

By the time I reached the office, details of President John F. Kennedy's assassination in Dallas, Texas, were trickling in. He was shot at 12:30 p.m., central time, and pronounced dead at 1 p.m. One hour and thirty-nine minutes later Vice President Lyndon B. Johnson was sworn in as president on Air Force One as it stood on the runway at Love Field in Dallas. Immediately after the oath-taking, the plane, with Mr. Kennedy's body on board, took off for Washington. The same question was on everyone's mind: "Who shot the president?"

The New York FBI office was put on standby.

*　*　*

When I was transferred from Terre Haute, Indiana, to New York City in 1959, it was initially a cultural shock. I went from a city of less than 60,000 to Manhattan, New York's third largest borough, with a population of well over 1 million.

But it was about more than numbers.

In Indiana the FBI office was directly across from Indiana State University. We had the use of the campus, where we took advantage of the arts, sports, and countless special events that interested the boys. I went to New York alone, leaving my family behind until I could locate housing. I naturally questioned why they would send me, a married man with three children, to New York City when the officials in Washington had other people who wanted to go to New York and were stuck in West Coast offices. But you do not question leadership. You bite your tongue and go about your business. Some agents, instead of accepting a transfer to New York submitted their resignations. That was not my style.

After I got my family established in a home at 2 Pine Tree Drive in Colonia, New Jersey, I finally settled in and began to enjoy my work in New York, knowing that I would meet all types of people. I had a long commute each day, but in those days you went with a car pool. With five or six men to a car, we became very close as you would imagine making that drive every day.

The FBI office was located at 201 East 69th Street in Manhattan, an exclusive area of East Side New York. Across the street was a high rise where actress Lucille Ball had her penthouse. Our building had about twelve stories. I was on the seventh floor. The FBI had full control of that space. There were no businesses. Our office was an open space, a big bullpen of detectives all sitting around in a big room. I had an assigned desk, but there were about twenty-five other agents around me. The supervisors all had offices. The Agent in Charge was on a different floor. The parking garage was twenty-five blocks away, north of our office. That's why you never saw FBI cars around. They were all in the garage. If we needed to respond to an emergency, we could not leave the building and jump into a car and take off with the siren screaming. Instead, we had to go to the corner, where the bus stop was located, and patiently wait for the next bus.

Today the FBI offices are in the Federal Building, but back then it was not unusual to spot Lucille Ball, Joan Rivers, Tony Bennett or other celebrities walking past the office on their way to their apartments. It was nice to be able to see a celebrity and tip your hat to them. I never stopped and encountered any of them because I knew they did not want to be bothered. They wanted other people to mind their own business.

There were also several Soviet Block missions in our neighborhood. The Soviet mission was only two blocks from the FBI office. The Cuban mission was probably four blocks away. As an FBI agent you never knew when you departed the office whether you were being tailed by Soviet or Cuban spies, so you were always careful going to the bus stop or to the subway, which was nearby, to make certain that you were not being followed.

If I had been followed by spies they would have discovered that Marie and I were frequently seen in the company of Felice Orlandi, a television and movie actor who often took on gangster roles, perhaps because of his Italian ancestry, a casting advantage. He was the spitting image of the stereotypical gangster. We were friends with him because he was married to Henryetta native Alice Ghostley, whom we befriended when we moved to New York. An accomplished actress, she was best known for her role as Aunt Esmerelda on the hit television series *Bewitched* and as Bernice in *Designing Women.*" Felice was best known for his gangster roles in the television series *FBI, Gunsmoke, and Hill Street Blues.*

When we got together, she would take us to Broadway shows and then we would go out to eat at places that she liked on Broadway. They had an apartment in Greenwich Village and they invited us there several times. They were always good to us. We'd go for walks at the university. We talked and laughed a lot. We just clicked, like you do when you are around a person that you're comfortable with. It was with regret that they moved to

52

Hollywood. We corresponded for a while, but that, too, came to pass because soon everyone got caught up in their own little world.

New York was a city that had it all. You could see more in one week there than most people would see in a lifetime. We took advantage of the Broadway shows, Radio City Music Hall, Time Square, the arts, the glitz, and much more. Because my work called for me to sometimes work the night shift, I would see things occurring on Times Square that most people would be aghast at witnessing. I also took advantage of seeing the Yankees, the Mets, the Jets and the New York Giants. Many surveillance assignments ended up in Yankee Stadium or other places of interest, so it was not unusual to visit a lot of interesting places when you were trailing different individuals. I always enjoyed seeing the Yankees because I was a fan of Mickey Mantle, having met the Mick in college when I was playing football.

One of the things I had a difficult time adjusting to was the snow. The snow was usually so heavy that we could never use the front door at home. We used the garage door as the entrance and constantly had to shovel the driveway. Our sons also had to make adjustments. When they arrived, they wore the blue jeans and boots that were traditional in Oklahoma. In New Jersey, traditional dress for teenagers was black pants and black leather jackets. It was like trying to mix oil and water. Recalls my son, Steve: "We looked different, and as a result, we were picked on and got into a number of fights." For Jim, the youngest, there are still vivid memories of the neighborhood bullies who targeted his older brothers. "One by one Steve and Stan would finish the fights the other guys started, usually whipping them pretty good," he recalls. "I remember one incident vividly where a guy called Steve out at our house on a Saturday, when we were all home. Dad allowed the fight to happen in our front yard, much to Mom's dismay, and Steve beat the guy up pretty badly, finally gaining respect from the neighborhood kids."

*   *   *

Most of us did not go home on the day of the Kennedy assassination. We stayed at the office, waiting for any assignment that might arise. It was a long night. Director Hoover proceeded under the mistaken assumption that there was a federal law against killing a president. Since 1934 there had been a federal law on the

53

books that made the killing of an FBI agent a federal offense, but there was no similar law involving the president. That meant that the president's murder was like any other murder in that the investigation fell under the jurisdiction of local authorities. It took a while to get all that straightened out.

Hoover was notified of the assassination only minutes after it happened by Dallas special agent in charge (SAC) Gordon L. Shanklin, who had two agents monitoring the president's motorcade on the police radio frequency. Hoover told Shanklin that he was in charge of the investigation and he proceeded accordingly; but the agent quickly learned that Texas authorities had classified the president's death as a felony murder, punishable under state law. That meant that the FBI could be involved in the investigation, but would not be in charge.

As all this was transpiring in Texas, I sat in the New York office with the other agents, supplementing the information we were receiving from headquarters with radio and television news broadcasts. Would the assassin's trail lead to New York? At this point, we simply didn't know.

Finally, at around 2 p.m. Central time, Hoover was notified that a suspect had been arrested by Dallas police. Lee Harvey Oswald was believed to have killed both the president and a Dallas police officer. There was an open file on Oswald in the Dallas FBI office, containing interviews that began when Oswald was contacted by Fort Worth agents upon his return to Texas from the Soviet Union. There were references in the file to Oswald's arrest in New Orleans for handing out "Fair Play for Cuba" leaflets. There was also information that he had angrily come into the FBI office in Texas to tell agents to stop questioning his wife.

That information in itself was enough for me to hit the New York City streets since I was assigned to the Cuban squad at that time. My job was pretty much that of a witness hunter. Who in the Cuban community had any knowledge of Lee Harvey Oswald? Was Kennedy's assassination an international plot hatched in the aftermath of the 1961 so-called "Bay of Pigs" invasion of Cuba by Cuban exiles living in the United States? Or was it related to the 1962 Cuban Missile Crisis that brought the world to the brink of nuclear war as President Kennedy faced off against Soviet Premier

Nikita Khrushchev over the removal of nuclear missiles from Cuba? At that point there were a lot more questions than answers.

With the interest in the Cuban Missile crisis and the interest in Fidel Castro, the Cuban squad was very active. I did not speak Spanish. However, I worked with a Spanish speaking agent because New York City, the Bronx, and Queens were replete with Cubans, many who loved Fidel Castro and many who detested Fidel Castro. You never knew where you stood with a particular individual until you did a background inquiry to determine what was going on with them.

The case was handed to FBI agent John J. O'Flaherty and I was assigned to assist him. O'Flaherty was perfect for the assignment. He was a former police officer with the New York Police Department. His grandfather, father, brother, all had been police officers in New York. Outside the office, I was on the same softball team with O'Flaherty when we won the city championship in the early 1960s, competing against other agency teams.

My job was to find people who were aware of any links between Oswald and the Cuban government. It was necessary to go back and trace, or attempt to trace, all the periods that the Oswalds spent in New York—their beliefs, Lee's propensity for violence, their associations—and track down anyone who knew them. It was also necessary to audit their funds. How did they live? Where did they spend their money? How did they receive funding? Why did they come to New York? Why did they leave?

We also had to contact persons associated with the Socialist Workers Party and the Communist Party, because Oswald had been in touch with different members who operated within those organizations in New York.

I had made some friends in the Cuban community and began with them. Had they ever heard of Oswald? I already knew from the file compiled by Dallas agents that Oswald and his mother had lived in New York from August 1952 until January 1954, when they left New York for New Orleans. Oswald completed the ninth grade and then left school to work for a year before enlisting in the U.S. Marines.

Oswald's New York years had been turbulent. He was raised by his mother without a father in the home. When he enrolled in a junior high school in the Bronx, the other students teased him because of his Texas accent. As a result, he began skipping school to stay at home by himself, where he spent his time reading magazines and watching television. Eventually truancy charges were brought against him alleging that he was "beyond the control of his mother." He was sent to Youth House, where children were held for psychiatric observation pending commitment to a training school.

Years later, the Warren Commission quoted the examining psychiatrist as reporting: "Lee has to be diagnosed as 'personality pattern disturbance with schizoid features and passive-aggressive tendencies.' Lee has to be seen as an emotionally, quite disturbed youngster who suffers under the impact of really existing emotional isolation and deprivation, lack of affection, absence of family life and rejection by a self involved and conflicted mother." Oswald was not sent to training school. Instead he was placed on probation, with a recommendation from the psychiatrist that Oswald needed a male therapist who could serve as a role model.

Oswald left behind a troubled history as a teenager in New York, but despite living on the Upper West Side of Manhattan in the Cuban section, neither he nor his mother ever could be linked to Cubans sympathetic to the Communist regime in Cuba. At least not that I was able to determine—and I left no stone unturned as I followed anything that even resembled a lead.

The Kennedy assassination investigation was the largest in the bureau's history. According to the report issued by the House Select Committee on Assassinations, more than 25,000 interviews were conducted by FBI agents, resulting in over 2,300 reports.

I was honored to have participated in that investigation. Not so honored were the seventeen agents censured by Hoover for their inability to connect the dots between Oswald and the assassination prior to the event, despite ample evidence that Oswald was a threat and had, in fact, once even threatened the FBI office in Dallas.

The FBI came under criticism for not sharing information about Oswald with the Secret Service, but at that time we were under strict orders from the top not to share information with other agencies. If the FBI office in Dallas had notified the Secret Service that Lee Harvey Oswald was a loose cannon in the city of Dallas, would it have made a difference? Possibly, but by the time the FBI office knew that Kennedy was coming to Texas, Oswald, who had served in the U.S. Marines and enjoyed a presumption of loyalty to the U.S., already had a plan in place and he would have been difficult to stop. Criticisms of the Bureau's handling of the investigation continued for years. One of the rumors was circulated by Mississippi Senator James O. Eastland, chairman of the Judiciary Committee, who warned that the CIA and the State Department had pointed a finger at the FBI by charging that Oswald was a confidential informant of the FBI. He also felt that the Secret Service blamed the FBI for the assassination. Hoover himself was so unhappy with the way the bureau handled the investigation he proclaimed the failures to be "a lesson to us all."

By the time the investigation in New York pertaining to Oswald had almost come to an end—it lasted for quite some time because you had the Commission asking the FBI for interviews and other work from the New York office and other field offices—I had been on the case for more than a year and a half, covering just about every lead coming in from the public and other sources.

By then I was ready to move on to an office in a smaller city, where I could have a Bureau car or walk to the office if I wanted to. But I questioned whether the Bureau would allow me to relocate from New York. Even if they did approve my request, I could not help but wonder what city would be a good fit for my family.

The assassination of President Kennedy was a dark day in the history of the United States, but those of us who worked on the investigation have always maintained that Lee Harvey Oswald was the lone gunman who acted on his own.

FBI poster showing, left to right, Michael Schwerner, James Chaney, and Andrew Goodman

4

MISSISSIPPI BURNING

From the mid-1950s onward, Mississippi was a seething cauldron of racial animosity, most of it centered on a combination of fears involving the political effects of black voter registration and white fears of interracial sex and intermarriage. What followed was an unprecedented series of hate crimes, the brutality of which was unknown in the civilized world.

It all began on July 26, 1948, when President Truman signed Executive Order 9981 abolishing racial segregation in the armed forces. Truman had called upon Congress to enact the changes, but Southern senators, particularly those from Mississippi, threatened a filibuster to block desegregation and Congress refused to act. He used the executive order as a last resort to ensure "equality of treatment and opportunity for all persons in the armed forces."

Six years later, the United Supreme Court bolstered Truman's decision by ruling in Brown v. Board of Education (1954) that racial segregation of children in public schools violated the Equal Protection Clause of the Fourteenth Amendment. That decision, in effect, put the U.S. Constitution on the side of racial equality and breathed fiery life into the civil rights movement.

Mississippi responded with heated rhetoric and a 1955 governor's race between former Governor Fielding L. Wright, who had a national reputation as a segregationist, and J. P. Coleman, a former judge who was viewed as the more moderate candidate. Throughout the summer of 1955, race was the major topic of conversation in the state. Into that heated witches brew walked 14-year-old Emmett Till of Chicago, who had come to Mississippi to visit family members. On a hot August day the youngster strolled into a country store and asked the 21-year-old married proprietor of the grocery for a date, prompting her to angrily follow him outside, presumably to get a pistol from a friend's car.

When she stepped out of the store, the youth whistled at her and then hurriedly fled without further incident. Subsequently, Till was kidnapped from a relative's house and savagely beaten and transported to the Tallahatchie River, where he was shot in the head with a .45-caliber automatic, his weighted body dumped into the river. Two weeks after Till's body was found, two men went on trial for the brutal murder. Both were quickly acquitted by an all-white, all-male jury.

As a national uproar over the savagery of the murder highlighted dismal race relations in Mississippi, the state legislature passed legislation creating a super-secret spy agency, the Mississippi State Sovereignty Commission, whose purpose was to block the federal government from enforcing racial equality in the state, using any means necessary.

A series of hate crimes followed: In 1959, a white lynch mob dragged a black man accused of rape from a Poplarville jail, shot him twice in the chest, and tossed his body into the Pearl River (no one was ever prosecuted); in September 1962, a black Air Force veteran by the name of James Meredith enrolled at the University of Mississippi under escort of federal marshals, prompting a riot that left two men dead; and in June 1963 Medgar Evers, the Mississippi field secretary for the NAACP, was assassinated with a .30-06 rifle when he pulled into the driveway of his Jackson home.

*   *   *

With the above-mentioned murders as a backdrop, three young men, Michael Schwerner, Andrew Goodman and James Chaney, all passionate about freedom, set out on Sunday, June 21, 1964, from Meridian, Mississippi, to investigate the ignoble burning of the Mount Zion Methodist Church in a rural area not far from Philadelphia. Goodman had arrived in Mississippi the night before from Oxford, Ohio. The other two men, Schwerner and Chaney, already had been targeted by the Mississippi State Sovereignty Commission for "subversive activities," a term used in Mississippi at that time by the media and elected officials to describe actions that encouraged blacks to exercise their constitutional right to vote.

All three men were commonly referred to in Mississippi as "civil rights workers," the phrase used in polite society. Beyond the glare of public scrutiny, the names given to individuals who encouraged blacks to register to vote were much more venomous. They became "agitators" or "communists" or "nigger lovers." The state made it as difficult as possible for blacks to vote by imposing a poll tax (money voters had to pay for the right to vote) and by requiring would-be voters to interpret sections of the U.S.

Constitution, the sole judge of the correctness of the interpretation being white election officials.

As the three men passed through Philadelphia in a blue station wagon, they attracted attention because Schwerner and Goodman were white and Chaney, who was behind the wheel, was black. It was a flagrant violation of a local social custom that prohibited whites and blacks from riding in the same car unless the black was wearing a chauffer's hat. Among those taking note of the blue car were Mississippi Highway Patrol officer H. J. Wiggs and his partner Robert Poe. Subsequently, I took a written statement from patrolman Wiggs that provides critical information about the last hours of the three men in the car. States Wiggs:

> **On June 21, 14:30 hours, we were parked east on Highway 16 when we saw a blue station wagon come by. When they saw the patrol car they slowed down. A few moments later Deputy Sheriff Cecil Price called us to come to the intersection of Beacon and Main. When we arrived we saw a blue station wagon with two white males and one negro male. They were changing a tire on the right rear, which was flat. I heard Deputy Price say that they were under arrest, the negro man for speeding and the other two white males for investigation. After they finished changing the flat, Deputy Price asked me if I would drive the station wagon and bring the negro male to the jail. The negro male got into the rear seat directly behind me. The negro didn't say anything to me nor did I say anything to him. I drove the car in and parked it beside the police station. I got out and brought the negro in front of the police station, where Deputy Sheriff Price took him from there. I went over in front of the jail and got into the patrol car. We went by the police station, got their names and description and went from there to the east side of the courthouse, where we talked to inspector King. From there we went back to normal patrolling—H. J. Wiggs.**

Price told the men that they could make a telephone call, but all three men declined to do so. They were fed a county dinner and held until 10:30 that night and then released after Chaney paid a twenty dollar fine set by a justice of the peace.

"Where you headed?" asked Deputy Price.

"Back to Meridian."

Price watched them drive onto Highway 45 and head toward Meridian. Then he got into his car and gave chase, soon joined by twenty additional men who had been alerted earlier in the day of their ultimate mission. The caravan followed the blue station wagon until it entered a desolate stretch of forest, at which point they stopped the car and surrounded it.

"Are you that nigger lover?" asked Alton Wayne Roberts as he pulled Schwerner from the car.

"Sir, I know how you feel," said Schwerner.

Roberts shot him pointblank, without explanation, and then pulled Goodman from the car, shooting him as well.

"You didn't leave me nothin' but a nigger," complained James Jordan. "At least I'll kill me a nigger."

At that point, Roberts turned to the other men and told them he would kill any of them who talked about what they had done, even if it turned out to be his own brother. The station wagon was set afire and abandoned. The bodies of the three civil rights workers were loaded into trucks and transported to a secret location where they were buried.

The next morning word spread throughout Philadelphia and Neshoba County that something bad had happened to the three men. Families and friends of the men notified authorities that they were missing. As news of the missing men made headlines across the nation, President Lyndon Johnson sent two hundred sailors from the naval base in Meridian, the nearest military installation, to assist in the search for the missing men.

The code name for the Philadelphia case and other violent civil rights violations then taking place in Mississippi was MIBURN, short for "Mississippi Burning." FBI Inspector Joe Sullivan was put in charge of the investigation. He was perfect for the job. He was not married. He devoted his life to the FBI and he was free to travel to any place that the bureau desired. He had the respect of the employees because of his knowledge and dedication to the FBI.

Joe became a dear friend of mine and when we had a riot at Jackson State University in 1970, at which people were killed and injured, I called on Joe for counseling and advice. He had just handled the deadly protest at Kent State University. What he told me certainly helped in our investigation at Jackson State.

Under Joe's direction, the Meridian bureau conducted the investigation of MIBURN in Philadelphia. In 1964 that bureau was staffed with John Proctor, Don Storker, Jack Rucker, Frank Watts, Don Cesar and Dan Bodine, each of whom conducted extensive investigations (Proctor, Rucker, Watts, and Bodine are now deceased).

On June 23, 1964 at 12:51 a.m., Storker received a telephone call from Harry Maynor, who at the time was the supervisor for the southern district of Mississippi (the field office had not yet opened in Jackson), informing him that he had information about the location of the blue station wagon. He explained that it had been discovered by a Native American in a swampy area of the Choctaw reservation. Maynor and Proctor then contacted the superintendent of the Choctaw agency in Philadelphia to get the information they needed to find the vehicle. Immediately after finding the vehicle, Proctor notified Joe Sullivan, who called Director Hoover.

On that same day, Hoover informed President Johnson that authorities had discovered the car driven by the three missing civil rights workers. "It had been set ablaze eight miles outside Philadelphia," explained Hoover. There was a pause. Then he continued, "Apparently, these men have been killed."

Johnson suggested that perhaps they had only been kidnapped.

Hoover promptly squashed that optimism and, perhaps to create a visual image, told him that the car was still burning when it was found. "We're going to have more cases like this down South. What's going to complicate matters is the agitators of the Negro [sic] movement."

Not long after talking to Hoover, Johnson decided to look elsewhere for someone to represent him in Mississippi. He sent former CIA director Allen Dulles to Jackson to meet with Erle Johnston, director of the Mississippi State Sovereignty Commission and publisher of the *Scott County Times*. Johnston was stunned that Dulles asked to meet with him instead of the governor, but the former CIA director wanted to get a straight-forward assessment of what the federal government could expect in Mississippi. Specifically, Dulles wanted to know the state's position on two organizations, the White Knights of the Ku Klux Klan and the Americans for the Preservation of the White Race.

Johnston considered Dulles's visit an encroachment on state's rights. In a memo to the governor, he tellingly wrote, "I informed them that the Sovereignty Commission had a few files on both of these organizations and some of their literature, but we had no cause for any concern or policies toward these groups so long as the groups and their members observed [your] policies of law and order."

When Dulles gave his report to the president, Johnson asked him to give his findings to Director Hoover over the telephone, so that he could listen on the speakerphone. With Hoover on the line, Dulles got right to the point: "You ought to review the number of agents that you have in that state . . . [authorities there] are not really going to enforce this business, I'm afraid, unless they have somebody looking over their shoulders."

Hoover said that would be difficult to do. He suggested that U.S. Marshalls, not FBI agents, should be sent to Mississippi to deal not just with the Mississippi Highway Patrol [known to have Klansmen on the payroll] but also with liberal religious organizations and black activists. That was more than Johnson could stand. He got on the line and said, "Maybe we can prevent some of these acts of terror by the very presence of your people."

Message delivered and received. Under orders of the President of the United States racial terrorists would go up against FBI agents, not U.S. Marshalls.

A few days later, the president telephoned Hoover and told him that the mother of Andy Schwerner, one of the missing civil rights workers, had been invited to the White House.

Annoyed by that news, Hoover sniffed, "She's a Communist, you know." It was his standard assessment of anyone he did not like. He went on to say, "I'm opening a main office, a full-time office at Jackson, Mississippi, with an agent in charge and a full staff as we would have in New York or San Francisco."

Pleased with that information, the president asked Hoover to go to Jackson to make clear the FBI's determination to fight race-based terrorism.

"Whatever you do, you're going to be damned," said Hoover. "Can't satisfy both sides."

That irritated the president so much that he made it clear that he didn't call Hoover to discuss his decision as much as he did to give him a direct order. He continued: "See how many people you can bring in there. You oughta put fifty, a hundred people, after this Klan, and study this from one county to another. I think their very presence may save us a division of soldiers." The president said he had stayed up half the night reading FBI intelligence reports on communists who "can't open their mouth without your knowing what they're saying."

Hoover agreed that was true.

"Now I don't want these Klansmen to open their mouths without your knowing what they're saying. Now nobody needs to know it but you, maybe, but we ought to have intelligence on that state."

Johnson left nothing to interpretation. He wanted Hoover to get just as tough on racist terrorists in Mississippi as he was on communist terrorists. Within hours after that conversation, Johnson signed the Civil Rights Act of 1964, a law that he had worked very hard to get through Congress.

Hoover dutifully went to Jackson, where he issued supportive statements about the FBI's new office in the city and had private meetings with Governor Johnson, state Attorney General Joe Patterson, highway patrol commissioner T. B. Birdsong, and the editors of the state's most conservative newspapers—*Jackson Daily News* editor Jimmy Ward, who had the reputation as the most conservative newspaper editor in the nation, and *Clarion-Ledger* editor Tom Hederman, who was equally conservative. He did not ask to meet with the Pulitzer Prize-winning Hodding Carter, editor of the moderate *Delta Democrat-Times* in Greenville, Mississippi, and one of a handful of editors in the state to argue for racial tolerance.

*   *   *

Charles Eddie Moore and Henry Hezekiah Dee, both nineteen, were like most teenagers in Meadville (population 594), Mississippi. There were few opportunities for work. Recreational opportunities were even scarcer. They could hardly go to the local restaurant to meet up with friends because everything in those days

65

was segregated—no blacks allowed. When it came to public facilities or white-owned businesses, they were always on the outside looking in.

Restrooms and water fountains bore signs—white men, white women, colored men, colored women. It was against the law for individuals of color to enter any public library.

On May 2, 1964, Moore and Dee, with limited options, set out in the blistering heat to see what everyone else was doing. They walked slowly along Highway 84, which also served as the town's main street.   There is no indication they felt a sense of danger. They were just taking a stroll in their neighborhood. If the Internet had been invented then—and they had known someone wealthy enough to own a computer—they might have received word of racial hate crimes in neighboring Pike County, where that year there were fourteen black homes bombed and four black churches destroyed or damaged by fire.

No one, not even the grandsons of slaves, wants to think that their hometown is a dangerous place in which to live. If you can't trust your hometown neighbors, who can you trust?

Moore and Dee had not walked far along Highway 84, occasionally sticking out their thumbs for a lift, when they spotted two white men in a white Volkswagen coming their way. They quickly dropped their hands, not wishing to solicit a ride from the likes of them. The car stopped anyway and a man later identified as twenty-nine-year-old James Ford Seale got out and falsely identified himself as an Internal Revenue Service agent. He ordered the teens into the cramped backseat of his car so that he could "talk" to them. No one was fooled by his awkward pretense.

Not until it became apparent that he was headed out of town toward Natchez, did they ask him to stop and let them out. He said no and then used a walkie-talkie to contact Klansmen in a pickup truck that was following them. Not far out of town, he turned off into the Homochitto National Forest, a 189,000-acre wildlife preserve about thirty miles from Natchez.

Soon the Volkswagen pulled off the road and stopped. Close behind was the pickup truck. Moore and Dee were told at gunpoint to get out of the car, after which they were taken to a tree where their wrists were bound with duct tape. After undergoing a severe beating, the two blood-soaked teens were forced back into the car and driven to a farm where they were crammed into the trunk of a red Ford that belonged to a Klansman from Natchez. They were transported, still alive, more than one hundred miles to an old channel of the Mississippi River named Palmyra Island. For years the strip of land, which was about twelve miles long and twenty-eight miles across, was associated with the Old Confederacy.

The plan all along had been to shoot them and then dump their bodies into the river, but Seale was concerned about the blood spillage that would involve, so it was decided they would weight them down with chains and a railroad rail and toss them into the water still alive. They took Dee first. His feet were wrapped with bailing wire and heavy Jeep parts were tied to his torso. Then he was loaded into the boat and paddled out into deep water and tossed overboard. Moore was forced to watch the entire procedure.

One can only imagine the terror he felt as they bound him and weighted him down and then took him out onto the water and pushed and pulled to roll him out of the boat. Did he feel the wetness of the water on his skin? Did he hold his breath as he sank into the muddy darkness?

Seale and his accomplices watched until the bubbles stopped.

FBI agent Joseph Sullivan   FBI Photo

5

THE MAGNOLIA STATE BECKONS

By the time the Lee Harvey Oswald investigation was winding down, I had become disillusioned with working in the New York office. In 1964, I spoke to the Special Agent in Charge, who, incidentally, had been the Special Agent in Charge in Terre Haute. I knew him well enough that I could sit down and talk to him about my concerns and frustrations. I told him I wanted a transfer and asked for his help in obtaining it.

I remember he said: "Ingram, you are in the Big Apple, the big leagues. Conduct yourself accordingly. I selected you when we were in the Indianapolis office in an effort to apprehend a top fugitive, someone who had been sought by the FBI for a long time. I selected you for a reason and you performed admirably. That's why I know you are a team player. So get back to work and continue to work at high efficiency and I know you will be happy."

I left his office disillusioned, but I remembered those words. They would come back to haunt me in an unexpected way. The problem with New York was that not everyone could afford to work there. These days if you are transferred to a major city, you are paid accordingly, much more than the individual who is working in a small office in a western or mountain state, where the living is not so expensive. The bottom line was that I could not work in New York and support my family. It created a hardship.

I will never, ever forget my good days in New York, but by 1964 I was making an effort to transfer out because of financial reasons. I had friends who had transferred to other places. Ernie Cochran and John Proctor had both transferred to Mississippi. Both called me and advised me to do my best to get to Mississippi: "This is the place you need to be." They convinced me to make the effort.

I was not from Mississippi. I had never thought about Mississippi, but the more I had telephone contact with both agents, the more enthusiastic I became about the possibility of getting a transfer. I knew Proctor extremely well. He had lived in New Jersey. We had a small group of agents that would meet with John

Proctor and Ernie Cochran and their families in their homes on Saturday evenings. We danced and laughed and relaxed. After they left New York, that pressure valve turned off like a faucet. I wanted more of that in my life. According to them, the only place I would find it was in Mississippi.

Finally, the powers that be gave in and granted my transfer. I would be arriving in Jackson, Mississippi, as the supervisor of the desk responsible for racial and security matters, civil rights, public accommodations and related matters such as voter registration and school integration.

At a little going away party in the New York office, I was chided by several speakers.

"Ingram, you've lost your mind."

"You have it made here in New York. Now you're going to a place and work, a place unknown to you, where you will work seven days a week?"

"Yes," I stubbornly affirmed.

"It's hot—there will be snakes."

They could think of every reason why I should not go to Mississippi, but I was so thrilled with the transfer that nothing they said affected me. Marie was in full concurrence. She had long wanted to leave New York because of the long hours I worked, made worse by a long commute home. I did not have sufficient time to spend with our sons. Truthfully, Marie raised our sons during the five years that we were in New York because we were apart hours during the day, hours during the evenings, and many times on the weekend I would get a call to return to work. She was very pleased to accept that transfer along with me.

Finally, the day came and we loaded up and left New York, heading for Jackson, Mississippi. After an uneventful trip, we arrived in Jackson and checked into the Alamo Plaza Motel on Highway 80. Then we went to a very nice restaurant for dinner. At one point during the evening, the owner came over and introduced himself. He could tell that we were not from this area and he wanted to know if we were passing through. I told him no, that we were in the process of moving to Jackson. I had been transferred here and we were looking forward to a new career in Jackson. He immediately asked my business. I told him I was an FBI agent assigned to the Mississippi office.

"Oh, you're one of the New York Yankees coming to save us."

I saw the smile on his face and knew I had to be prepared.

"That is not our intent," I explained. "I am here to work for the government and I'm anxiously looking forward to starting a new career and my family is very pleased to be in Mississippi."

"You're not from Mississippi?"

"No, but we will be from here on."

He smiled and went behind his desk. Soon he returned with a map of the city.

"I want you to have a map," he said. "I want to at least tell you what I think you should do right away. Look for housing in the northeast section of Jackson. They have better schools, better housing. This is the area where you want to be."

Though it was very nice of him to offer his advice, I was noncommittal and said, "Mister, we do not know anything about Jackson." Then I thanked him. The next morning I reported to the Jackson office, but many times thereafter I stopped in the restaurant and talked to the gentleman and gave him an update and surprisingly we became very good friends.

* * *

Veteran agent Roy K. Moore, who was hand-picked by Hoover, was named Special Agent in Charge (SAC) of the new Jackson office. A native of Hood River, Oregon, he grew up in Illinois and joined the U.S. Marines, where one of his duties was to train new FBI agents in the use of firearms. After leaving the Marines, he joined the FBI and attended the University of Miami while stationed in Florida. As head of the Jackson office, Moore named Neil Welch the assistant agent in charge and Joe Sullivan was put in charge of the Neshoba County investigation into the murders of Goodman, Schwerner and Chaney.

Driving around Jackson that day I remarked what an outwardly beautiful city it was at that time. Its population was almost 75 percent black, but all the businesses I came in touch with were white owned and the black presence was almost invisible. Mississippi had the reputation of lynching black people, generally mistreating black people, more so than any other state in the union. The murder of Emmett Till in 1955 was just one of the black eyes of Mississippi. The riot at the University of Mississippi during the integration of the university in 1962 was another. Then there was the 1959 lynching of Charles Mack Parker, a black male who had been accused of raping a white woman, and the murder of civil rights leader Medgar Evers. These were just some of the cases that received national and international media attention.

There were so many things that needed immediate action. When I called John Proctor, who was stationed in Meridian, to tell him that I had been transferred to Jackson, John was elated. I also called Ernie Cochran, who was the first to greet me when I arrived at the Jackson office. Ernie reminded me that I had been the first person to greet him when he was transferred to New York City.

Ernie and I had been new agents in training in 1956, so we had a long friendly relationship that existed long after I retired. I was surprised when I arrived in Mississippi how many agents that I already had worked with and knew.

Some of the agents that had been transferred to Jackson refused to go and asked for reassignment. Some that refused were asked to resign from the Bureau. Others were sent on temporary duty for three to six months.

Neil Welch, who was in charge of all criminal violations in Mississippi, was a tough administrator. Later in his career, he was the premier expert on organized crime for the FBI. Neil served in most of the large FBI field offices and he was a friend of mine for many years. When I first arrived, Neil had several agents, including myself, set up a nighttime stakeout on a hog farm on the Mississippi River. We were looking for a fugitive bank robber who was involved in a shootout in which a person had been killed.

Moving in that night on a hog farm, you guessed it, we had to sleep with the hogs. Raised on a farm the way I was, I don't recall ever wallowing in hog muck, but we did it that night. The sad part about it was that after staying there all night our fugitive did not show. He was later apprehended at another location.

We had some colorful characters in our investigative teams. Sometimes we were asked to investigate violations of a new public accommodation law that most Southern states did not recognize. We called that team the crapper squad. It was a group of agents who fanned out across the state to investigate the so-called "separate but equal" accommodations in hotels, motels, restaurants, gas stations, any type of establishment that had separate facilities for blacks and whites. At that time, Mississippi had separate restrooms for whites and blacks, separate swimming pools, separate drinking fountains, and separate schools for whites and blacks.

The FBI frequently got complaints that restaurants refused to serve black people, so when that happened it was necessary to conduct an investigation. It was not unusual to see facilities that claimed they were separate but equal. But no way was that the case. You would come across gas stations or restaurants or other public accommodations where you had restrooms for white men only, white women only, and then restrooms marked "colored." In the colored restrooms, you'd have the doors off, no toilet seats. You would see dirty facilities for the black community and clean facilities for the whites. There'd be public drinking fountains, but they would be designated as "white" or "colored." In many instances, the colored drinking fountains never functioned.

I had agents tell me, "I didn't join the FBI to check crappers to see if the toilets worked, or to see if we had toilet seats in white restrooms and no toilet seats in colored restrooms." Many agents told me that if their friends back East asked what type of work they did, they could not tell them that they were working a hideous murder case. No, they would have to tell them that they were taking photographs of crappers in hot, 100-degree weather.

It was not a very good job, but one which the U.S. Department of Justice expected us to perform. You can't imagine all the jawing, the yelling, the jokes by local citizens, as agents conducted their inquiries in Delta towns such as Midnight, Silver City, and Beulah. There were always two agents involved—one taking photographs, and one watching the back of the agent taking the photographs. Naturally, the agents bore the wrath of locals, being called Yankee Communists, Yankee bastards, Yankee sons of bitches, always followed by some form of the declarative, "Yankee go home." But it all went with the job.

I never suspected after arriving in Mississippi that school integration would also take a toll on my own children. Marie and I never discussed that possibility because we were unaware of what we would face. At the time we left New York, Stan and Steve were thirteen and they had many friends that they had developed in New York. They also had girlfriends. They truly regretted leaving, knowing they would probably never see those individuals again.

Our third son, Jim, who was eight years old, felt the same way and was ill-prepared by us for the tumult of school desegregation. Everything went smoothly the first five years, but then in 1969 Jim and a small group of white students were bused from their schools in northeast Jackson to all-black schools in the west section of Jackson. Not long after the busing began, a disturbance arose and classes were dismissed because of fighting between white and black students. I received a call informing me of an incident at a school and I immediately realized that it was the school that young Jim had been bused to.

When I arrived on the scene, the Jackson police were already restoring order. I looked for my son and could not find him. I was told that most of the white students had left and were walking home. I looked for Jim, but I could not find him. I found some of his friends and they told me they had not seen him.

After searching for about an hour, I found him with some other boys walking back home. It was a trip of several miles. None of them had been injured, but my son Jim was told by other students that if he returned to school someone might pick a fight with him. That statement was made not only to him, but to others. Of course, my son returned to school and there were other incidents, but I must say, my son was stronger than I was because he ended up with a good education, got a degree from the University of Mississippi and graduated from the Harvard Business School Advanced Management Program.

Today Jim recalls that the situation improved greatly after the initial shock of transferring to a majority black school. "It did get better for me because I played the drums in the band and the band leader selected two section leaders for the drum section, being me and a black kid. The drum section must have had over twenty members, most of whom were black. I had taken drum lessons and was good at playing the rudiments, whereas the black guys were just naturally good at the beat. I helped create some of our drum solos, drum line style, so I actually made a few friends and allies in the process. I was scared in the first month of the transition, but it got much better."

Steve's recollections of transferring from a New Jersey school to a Mississippi school are similar to those he experienced moving from Oklahoma to New Jersey, except they were in reverse order.

When they moved to Mississippi it was the Ingram boys who were wearing black pants and black leather jackets and the Mississippi boys who were wearing blue jeans.

"So, there we were, me and Stan wearing black leather jackets going to Chastain Junior High," he recalls. "What happened? Our first day at school, some kids picked a fight. We got through it fine. Actually, we have very good memories of those years."

My sons weren't the only ones at risk. We had many threats made against agents. I had threats, of course, on my life because I was very involved, very high profile. Roy Moore had threats against his life. In one particular incident, the Klan threatened to bomb his house. We set up a day-and-night surveillance of his home. Nothing ever happened. No arrests were made, but we always had to be prepared.

Mr. Moore's two daughters both married FBI agents, so we were concerned about them as well. We had incidents in which agents were threatened and poisonous snakes placed in their mailbox. You always had to look under your car before you started it, whether it was a personal or bureau car, to make sure there were no bombs attached. The Klan in Mississippi had some individuals who were very knowledgeable on concocting bombs.

* * *

About ten weeks after Dee and Moore were drowned on July 12, 1964, a couple was fishing in the old Mississippi River backwater at Palmyra Island, when the woman hooked something that required her to pull her line up out of the water to free her fishing hook. On the other end of the line was a human vertebra. Another line brought up another part of the body that contained some items in the pants pocket. She wasted no time notifying the sheriff, who in turn called the FBI, thinking the remains might belong to one of the missing civil rights workers.

Before FBI agents arrived, the sheriff called Sheriff Rainey in Philadelphia to let him know that they probably had found the missing civil rights workers. Rainey promptly turned the telephone over to Deputy Cecil Price who led the sheriff to think that might be the case.

In October FBI agents and investigators from the highway patrol met with the U.S. Navy mine defense lab out of Panama City, Florida. Navy divers arrived at the Palmyra Landing to discuss diving operations to recover the upper bodies of the men and any other objects they could find. They explained they were going to run a land-to-bottom search and the lines would be run across the river and two navy divers would search an area about five feet from the north bank to the south bank.

Our agents began their operation at Parker's Landing, which was owned by Ernest Parker. A search warrant was given to Parker because he had refused entry to his land without one. Divers found shirts, a skull, and miscellaneous bones, along with the Jeep motor block. They were all found together in the same place. In another area, bones, railroad ties, chains and a T-shirt were discovered.

Robert Lee Parker, Ernest's brother, was interviewed by FBI agents (Ernest refused to be interviewed) and said he and his brother owned 10,000 acres on the island and owned land on the Louisiana side as well. They used a steel barge to ferry trucks, cattle, and cars to the island. He lived several miles from the landing and his brother lived in Natchez. All of the recovered items, including the Jeep block, were transported to Jackson and then sent to the FBI lab in Washington D.C. Riding in the back of the truck to Jackson with the bodies was a very painful experience.

It soon became apparent from the items found in the pockets of the remains that the bodies discovered in the river were not the missing civil rights workers, but instead were Moore and Dee. A Klansman named Ernest Gilbert told FBI agents that he had information that would be helpful. He pointed a finger at Seale's brother, Jack, and another Klansman who had bragged about the murders. He also disclosed that Seale was concerned that his fingerprints might be on the duct tape used to bind the teens. It was not until November 6, 1974, that James Seale and Charles Edwards were arrested by FBI agents and sheriff's deputies and charged with killing Moore and Dee. They were taken to Jackson for questioning and then returned to Meadville. In the car, FBI agent Leonard Wolf discussed the crime with Seale.

"We know you did it. You know you did it. The Lord knows you did it."

"Yes," Seale sneered, "but I'm not going to admit it. You are going to have to prove it."

Seale was not overly concerned that he would ever pay for his crimes. No white man in Mississippi had ever been successfully prosecuted during the civil rights era for killing a black man. He knew that despite the evidence gathered by the FBI, the local district attorney would look the other way. As it turned out, the district attorney dropped all charges against Seale on the grounds that the case was "greatly prejudiced" against the defendants.

After Seale and Edwards were initially released in early 1965, the Klan again knew they could do just about anything they wanted, even though there was a large contingent of FBI agents in Natchez and Franklin County conducting investigations. The black community was not satisfied and demonstrations and marches became an every weekend occurrence in Natchez.

I was receiving information from some excellent black informants that invitations were going out that everyone who could get free should come to Natchez to assist in demonstrations. J. T. Robison was the chief of police in Natchez and he worked closely with our agent Billy Bob Williams, who was assigned to handle the local Natchez matters. The civil rights demonstrations, along with the Klan demonstrations and rallies in the parks on weekends, created a volatile situation.

Robison asked for and received National Guard help. At the same time, after all the publicity about Moore being a student at Alcorn, a state-supported college, trouble began to erupt on the campus. A major riot broke out and the Mississippi highway patrol sent hundreds of troopers onto the campus to quell the violence. It was not a pleasant thing to see.

Some students were hurt, but none were killed. I well remember the event because we were on campus with the highway patrol and other law enforcement contingents, watching the students being dispersed. After watching those who had been hit, I can well remember an older black lady, yelling out, "Has anyone seen my red shoe? I lost a red shoe. Help me look for my red shoe."

This was right in the midst of some students who had had their shirts ripped from their bodies. It was a chaotic situation. Members of the justice department were there as observers and members of the press from all over the country were there, reporting on what they actually saw.

Chief Robison had his hands full because it was not a violation of law to be a Klansman. On a Saturday you would see Klansmen dressed in their robes without the hoods handing out pamphlets inviting spectators to attend Klan rallies. Then you had the black community handing out leaflets for different rallies. You had to remember that Natchez was a tourist attraction, with the Mississippi Delta Queen and other boats docking, filled with tourists who undoubtedly found all this interesting as they took photos of Klansmen in their sheets, standing around as if they were extras on a movie set.

One of my partners was Jim Awe. He was a tremendous photographer and he took photos of the Klansmen as they took photos of us. It was quite a scene to see. But all this time the FBI headquarters in Washington wanted detailed reports on the riot at Alcorn. They wanted detailed reports on all our interviews, so you had to dictate your observations and get everything on the books immediately. Roy Moore knew it would take seven days a week. He knew you had to keep people busy. I learned from the master.

A crisis was brewing around the Natchez area because the black community was beginning to exert itself. By then they had the Deacons for Defense, a black militant group that was very organized in Louisiana and somewhat in Mississippi and was getting stronger by the day. That became obvious when the riots broke out on the Alcorn campus. Therefore you had two groups going at each other—the Klan and the Deacons for Defense.

* * *

Once the burned-out station wagon driven by the missing Neshoba County civil rights workers was located near Philadelphia, it was essential that the investigation slip into high gear to locate the three men. Jay Cochran, an expert in firearms examinations, tool marks, explosives, and other related laboratory subjects, was dispatched from FBI headquarters to Mississippi to examine the vehicle and the items found inside.

Also on the scene was FBI agent John Proctor and eighteen other FBI agents, along with Andrew Hopkins, an investigator for the Mississippi State Sovereignty Commission. Neshoba County Sheriff Lawrence Rainey asked Proctor who had reported the location of the vehicle. Proctor told him, quite accurately, that the call had come to the office in Meridian, but he refused to reveal the identity of the informant.

Sheriff Rainey pulled Hopkins aside and told him that he was upset with the way the FBI had treated his wife, who was in the hospital recovering from surgery.

"What did they want?" asked Hopkins.

"They wanted to know where I was on the evening the civil rights workers disappeared."

Hopkins filed a report with his superiors, who did not share information with the FBI, stating that Rainey was a suspect in the church burning that had instigated the visit from the civil rights workers and possibly in the disappearance of the missing men. Wrote Hopkins in his report: "FBI agents questioned him for a period of approximately three hours Tuesday afternoon, June 30, and indicated by their questions that he was a suspect and knew more than he was telling about the case. The sheriff stated that near the end of the interview, an agent said to him: 'Now come on sheriff and tell us what you did with those people.' One agent asked the sheriff if he was a member of the KKK and, of course, the sheriff denied being a member of the Klan as he has repeatedly denied it to me since the beginning of this investigation. At one point, the sheriff stated that an agent pointed his finger at him and said: 'Don't you defy the federal government!'"

As the investigation continued, a temporary FBI headquarters was set up in Room 18 of the Delphia Motel in Philadelphia. The agents' first priority was locating a witness to the car burning, someone who would become an informant for the FBI. That process took about one month.

In late July 1964, FBI Agent Glenn Ing and a second agent were dispatched from FBI headquarters in Washington to Meridian with a nondescript package. They were instructed to personally hand the package to Inspector Joe Sullivan and no one else. They were told to keep the package in their possession at all times. They were not told what was in the package.

Sullivan took delivery of the package, which was filled with cash, and surreptitiously delivered the contents to an informant who then revealed the location of the bodies of the civil rights workers. U.S. Attorney General Nicholas Katzenbach asked to be informed of the identity of the informant, but Sullivan declined, citing the risk it would pose to his informant's life. If this sounds contrary to the procedure I outlined previously in the book, whereas at least two agents always knew the identity of an informant, it is because the stakes in this case were so high that Sullivan was not pressured to tell more than he wanted to tell.

FBI Agent Cochran, who already was in Mississippi to search for clues in the station wagon, was told on August 4 to accompany a convoy of heavy earth-moving equipment from Jackson to a dam that was located off Highway 21, just six miles from the Neshoba County courthouse. Before setting out on that mission, Cochran flew over the property in a helicopter to precisely fix the location of the dam based on the information that Sullivan had supplied to him. Cochran alone made the decision about where to dig. He chose a point 155 feet from the west end of the dam.

After an all-day search, three bodies were recovered and transported to the University Medical Center in Jackson, for further identification. Cochran noted that he had found a Selective Service card for Andrew Goodman on one corpse and one for Michael Schwerner on his body. Cochran accompanied the bodies to Jackson and was present during the autopsy. Also attending the autopsy was the Neshoba County coroner, Sheriff Rainey, who had driven back from the Gulf coast the night before; Deputy Price; a private practicing pathologist, Dr. Featherstone, as well as a photographer from the Mississippi Highway Patrol. It was during that process that the third body found was positively identified as James Chaney. As expected, it was discovered that all three men died as a result of gunshot wounds.

When the Sovereignty Commission investigator, Andrew Hopkins, heard the news that the bodies had been found, he rushed back to Neshoba County to see for himself what was happening. Not far from the dam, Hopkins encountered a roadblock manned by two Mississippi highway patrolmen. They told him the bodies had been removed and were on the way to University Hospital in Jackson, where the autopsy would be performed.

Hopkins was told that Deputy Sheriff Price had been offered one million dollars by the FBI for evidence that would solve the case. Noted Hopkins in his report: "The agents told Price that he could 'leave Mississippi with that kind of money and buy a cattle ranch in Wyoming.'" What most interested Hopkins was whether authorities knew the caliber of the weapon that was used in the killings. His source at the highway patrol could not speak to that, but he did know that there was one bullet in Schwerner's body, one bullet in Goodman's body, and three bullets in Chaney's body.

Because the FBI is an investigative agency, not a prosecutorial one, it collects evidence and then turns it over to the prosecuting authority that has jurisdiction over the case—local, state or federal. However, in this case the FBI did not release evidence to the local district attorney because there was a suspicion within the bureau that two county officials were involved in the crime.

Neither did the agency turn the evidence over to Mississippi Governor Johnson or Mississippi Attorney General Patterson. The last time they'd shared evidence with Mississippi state officials—in the infamous Poplarville lynching case in which a black man accused of raping a white woman was dragged by a mob from a county jail in full view of townspeople and driven to a bridge where he was murdered and his body tossed into the river—no effort was made to pursue prosecution. Because they didn't trust Mississippi officials to uphold the U.S. Constitution and faithfully prosecute the case on murder charges under state law, the FBI turned the evidence over to the U.S. Justice Department to prosecute under federal civil rights laws.

* * *

On December 4, 1964, to the surprise of state officials, we sent enough FBI agents to Neshoba County to arrest twenty-one men charged with violating the civil rights of the Philadelphia civil rights workers. Included in the roundup were Sheriff Lawrence Rainey, Chief Deputy Cecil Price, and Edgar Ray Killen, a thirty-nine-year-old Baptist preacher from Union.

The men were taken before a federal commissioner in Meridian, where they were formally charged, and then sent to the naval base in Meridian, where they were held in isolation so that they could not receive visitors. Four days later, the commissioner, a grandmotherly woman named Esther Carter, dropped charges against most of the men. The office of commissioner, by the way, is no longer in existence, replaced by the office of U.S. magistrate. It is safe to say that federal prosecutors were stunned by her decision. At about that same time, a second commissioner in Biloxi released another defendant. That left only two defendants, both of whom were soon released.

Prosecutors were sent back to square one.

About one month later, prosecutors went before a federal grand jury in Jackson and obtained indictments on eighteen of the twenty-one men originally charged. The judge who awaited the case was Harold Cox, the hand-picked choice of U.S. Senator James Eastland who had been responsible for his appointment to the bench. Whatever jubilation the prosecutors felt over the indictments was quickly dashed by Cox who dismissed all the felony indictments against the men, ruling that they could only be charged with misdemeanors.

The Justice Department appealed Judge Cox's decision to the United States Supreme Court. Most Mississippians assumed the case was over, yet another victory for states' rights. But it didn't turn out that way. In March 1966 the Supreme Court overturned Judge Cox's decision. Defense attorneys filed a motion to have the grand jury indictments thrown out on the grounds that the jury members had been improperly chosen.

Prosecutors shocked everyone by agreeing. Judge Cox dismissed the indictments, a decision that led the defendants to believe that they had gotten off scot-free.

But it was only a tactical move. The Justice Department regrouped and added new defendants to the case, including KKK "Imperial Wizard" Sam Holloway Bowers and former Neshoba County Sheriff Hop Barnett. In February 1967, prosecutors went before a new grand jury and obtained indictments on the original conspiracy charges. Eight months later eighteen defendants went on trial in Judge Cox's courtroom on charges of conspiracy to deprive Goodman, Chaney, and Schwerner of their civil rights. It seems like ridiculous charges for such a heinous crime, but only the state could prosecute the men for murder and it steadfastly had refused to do so.

Heading up the prosecution team from the Justice Department was John Doar, a veteran of the forced integration of Ole Miss. This was the first case the Civil Rights Division had ever tried in Mississippi, and to make matters even more dramatic Doar announced before the trial even began that he planned to retire at the conclusion of the trial. In opposition to Doar was every practicing attorney in Neshoba County. Eleven lawyers. In the minds of many Mississippians, it was the Civil War all over again.

As serious as the trial was, it was not without its moments of humor. Minnie Lee Herring and her husband lived at the Neshoba County jail in Philadelphia. She operated the jail with her husband and she was on duty at the jail on June 21, 1964, when Deputy Cecil Price brought Goodman, Chaney and Schwerner in and booked them for speeding.

At the trial she was asked if the three individuals gave her any trouble while in jail.

"Not a bit in the world," she answered.

During cross-examination by an attorney for the defense, she was asked by the attorney if she was related to him.

"You know I am," she answered. "You're my son-in-law."

With that the Judge Cox intervened. "Let's keep on track and not ask questions when it's not necessary."

Later, the same attorney got into trouble with Judge Cox while he was cross-examining the Rev. Charles Johnson, a Meridian minister. John Doar had questioned Rev Johnson about Michael Schwerner, his voter registration efforts, how he knew Schwerner, etc. The attorney, in his cross, asked Rev Johnson, "Did not Schwerner advocate young male negroes to sign statements agreeing to rape a white woman once a week during the hot summer of 1964?"

The federal prosecutor objected.

Judge Cox said he was going to allow the witness to answer that question.

Rev. Johnson asked the defense attorney if he would repeat the question.

The attorney responded, "I asked you if it's not true that you and Mr. Schwerner didn't try to get young Negro males to sign statements that they would rape one white woman a week during the hot summer of 1964?"

Johnson answered, "No never."

Judge Cox then said, "Counsel you ought to have a good basis for a question like that. It would be highly improper to ask a question without a basis. I look forward to seeing a basis for that question in this record."

The attorney said, "Your honor, please, it's just a note passed on to me by someone else."

Judge Cox asked, "Who is the author of that question?"

"Your honor, I don't know."

Judge Cox said, "I want to know right now who the author of that question is. Which one of you passed the question up?"

A second attorney said, "It was passed to me and then I passed it on."

Cox asked, "Who wrote the question?"

"Brother Killen wrote the questions. One of the defendants."

"Judge Cox said, "You mean one of the defendants wrote that question? All right, I'm going to expect some basis for that question since counsel has adopted one of defendant's questions and if there is no basis for it, then when we get through I'm going to say something about it."

"Your honor—please!"

"I'm not going to allow a farce to be made of this trial and everyone had better get that through their heads, including every one of the defendants."

"Your honor, please, I will be more careful about the questions asked. I will be diligent in obeying the court."

Judge Cox responded, "I don't understand a question such as that. Don't appreciate it and I will say something when we get through with this trial. You cannot be just as reckless as you want in asking questions like that. I'm surprised at a question like that coming from a preacher. I'm talking about Killen or whatever his name is."

Judge Cox set the tone of the trial that day. In the course of the trial I got to know Judge Cox extremely well. Later, when I was working again in New York, Judge Cox and Mrs. Cox would come to New York and visit and I would get together with them for dinner. Cox was as responsible as anyone during the trial that the defendants had to answer for themselves.

* * *

Developing informants and co-operative witnesses is one of the most difficult jobs a person can have. Many times you spend days, long hours, long nights, attempting to convert an individual as an informant. Former agent Roy Mitchell was able to convince Sergeant Wallace Miller, a 20 year veteran of the Meridian police department, to assist the FBI back in 1964. Miller, who is now deceased, gave agent Mitchell considerable information over a period of time about the Klan, Bowers, and some of the defendants on trial in 1967. Mitchell convinced Miller to testify in the trial and Miller told the jurors about other Klansmen and about meeting with preacher Killen on several occasions in their back room and at their kitchen table at Miller's home in Meridian.

Killen also furnished background to the murder plot to Miller and explained how he got together Klansmen to carry out the killings of Goodman, Schwerner, and Chaney. Miller also revealed that Schwerner had been approved for elimination by Imperial Wizard Bowers. Miller gave the court background on the burning of Mount Zion Methodist Church on June 16, 1964, a few days before the killings. Miller's information was very revealing.

Another source, Rev. Delmar Dennis, was developed by former agent John Martin and FBI agent Don Caesar. Rev. Dennis was extremely helpful to the FBI. The fact that he knew Killen well, that Killen swore him into the Klan in 1964 at the Cash Salvage Store in Meridian, made him an important witness. Dennis explained what Killen meant when he used the word "elimination" (it meant to kill a person). According to Preacher Killen, any project carried out by the Klan had to be approved. The approval meant it had to come from Sam Bowers.

Dennis also explained how he and Bowers spoke by code. Rev Dennis, who is deceased, also talked about gathering snakes to use against civil rights workers. Sergeant Miller, with his long-time service in the police department, and Rev. Delmar Dennis, with his knowledge of the Klan, were dominating witnesses and they were very impressive.

James Jordan, now deceased, furnished detailed information to FBI agents Proctor and Richard Harrelson on who was involved in the killing of Goodman, Schwerner and Chaney. Jordan admitted his participation with the group and Killen's participation on gathering the group to do a job in Neshoba County. Jordan convinced Klansman Alton Wayne Roberts to stop and get some gloves before the killing. Jordan explained that Rev. Killen went into detail about the three individuals being locked up and how they had to rush to get there. Jordan, as a cooperating witness, testified that he gave information to Proctor, Harrelson and other agents. He also was a very convincing witness.

Horace Doyle Barnett was interviewed by FBI agents Henry Rask and James Wooten in Los Angles in 1964 and furnished a signed confession setting out the entire scenario of the crime and those involved. This was the frosting that enabled the FBI and the Justice Department to bring these individuals to justice. Evidence pointed out that after the three had been released from the jail that evening, Price and a group totaling twenty stopped them and Alton Wayne Roberts pulled Schwerner from the car, with Roberts asking, "Are you that nigger lover?"

Roberts shot Schwerner and then turned, pulling Goodman from the car, shooting him, too, killing them both. James Jordan said, "You did not leave anything but a nigger, but at least I'll kill me a nigger." Roberts told the group, not to talk or he would kill anyone who talked, "even if it's my brother." That's when the bodies of the three civil rights workers were taken to the dam site, buried and their station wagon set afire and left abandoned.

In his closing argument, Doar praised the courage of the three FBI witnesses who had testified for the government, saying that they were essential in solving the case: "Midnight murder in the rural area of Neshoba County provides few witnesses."

After deliberating for one day, the jury returned to the courtroom and explained that they were deadlocked. Judge Cox told them to go back and try again. The next day the jury returned with verdicts. To the surprise of everyone, when the first verdict was read—"We the jury, find the defendant Cecil Ray Price not guilty"—there was a collective gasp in the courtroom.

The jury foreman continued speaking. "I'm sorry your honor, may I start over?"

Judge Cox nodded his approval.

"We, the jury, find the defendant Cecil Ray Price *guilty* of the charges contained in the indictment."

Guilty verdicts were announced for six additional defendants: Jimmy Arledge, Jimmy Snowden, Sam Bowers, Alton Wayne Roberts, Billy Wayne Posey, and Horace Doyle Barnette. The remaining eight defendants were acquitted, including Sheriff Lawrence Rainey. The jury was unable to reach a verdict on three defendants, including Edgar Ray Killen and former Sheriff Hop Barnett.

At the sentencing on December 29, Judge Cox gave ten year sentences to Roberts and Bowers; Posey and Price each received six years. And Barnette, Snowden, and Arledge each got three years. Judge Cox explained the sentences this way: "They killed one nigger, one Jew, and a white man. I gave them all that I thought they deserved."

The defendants immediately filed an appeal and went home on bond, where they stayed for three years as the case made its way through the appeal process, all the way to the U.S. Supreme Court. In 1970, the High Court refused to hear the case and finally Sam Bowers, Cecil Price and the others were sent to prison, where they served sentences, not for murder, but for violating the civil rights of the three murdered victims.

I have always been haunted by the fact that the three murdered men had been offered a telephone call by their jailers, but declined to take advantage of the offer. I don't know what their thinking was. Some thought they were not in harm's way in Neshoba County and would return to Lauderdale County. But they should have made that telephone call. A lot of lessons were learned from that day. After that, any civil rights workers who came to Mississippi knew, if they were arrested, to immediately make that telephone call.

Jim Ingram examining evidence taken from Klansman's home

6

CODE NAME DABURN

On the evening of January 10, 1966, Vernon Dahmer, his wife, Ellie, and their children came under a vicious firebomb attack at their home in Forrest County, Mississippi. As Dahmer desperately rushed to get his wife and children out of the burning house, they came under gunfire from terrorists as they exited, forcing them back inside the smoke-filled building.

Their would-be killers wanted the most painful death possible for them as smoke whirled about the house and the stores next door, which also had been set afire. As Dahmer bravely laid down a hail of gunfire from inside the house, his wife and children managed to escape, though not without suffering the effects of the fire, especially 10-year-old Bettie, who experienced painful burns.

No one was wounded in the shootout and the assailants faded away into the night, allowing Dahmer to flee from the burning building before it was consumed. But the effects of the fire were more devastating than anyone realized. He died the following day at a local hospital, a victim of cowardly nightriders.

Dahmer was one of the most successful African Americans in the county. A successful businessman, he owned a store, a sawmill, a 200-acre farm, and a planing mill. He was the music director and Sunday school teacher at the Shady Grove Baptist Church. He served several terms as president of the Forrest County Chapter of the National Association for the Advancement of Colored People (NAACP) and he was active in voter registration drives.

Dahmer's favorite saying was, "If you don't vote, you don't count." It was a phrase he repeated on his deathbed, knowing full well the identity of his killers, if not by name then by reputation. That one phrase was the basis of countless murders and bombings in the South. It was the right to vote that inflamed the passions of white racists who saw black voter participation as the doomsday knell for white supremacy.

The FBI had a pretty good idea who was behind the murder—everyone in the black community knew that the KKK had played a role—but we needed evidence to instigate a successful prosecution. We were taught in the FBI to do the investigation, gather the facts, present the data to the prosecutor, and then step out. That was a different situation in Mississippi because we were gathering facts that the state should have gathered and we were then presenting these facts to the authorities and then the authorities were turning their backs and saying, "not enough evidence." Then you had some Klansmen who were deputies or police officers and they just loved the fact that the state could refuse to prosecute based on information gathered by the FBI. It was most difficult and frustrating when the state would not follow through and prosecute.

The FBI had no jurisdiction whatsoever to investigate civil rights murders in Mississippi, but when the president orders the director of the FBI to solve the cases, no matter what the cost, that's a pretty good instruction from the most powerful person in the world and so we did. That's what irritated so many of the citizens of Mississippi. They were smart enough to know that. Their lawyers had told them they didn't have to talk to the FBI and could tell us to leave their property. And they were correct. That's what made it so difficult.

Following the death of Vernon Dahmer, a large contingent of FBI agents, highway patrol officers, and sheriff's deputies began their investigation. FBI agent Robert E. Lee, assigned to Laurel, Mississippi, in Jones County, promptly came up with information indicating that Sam Bowers, the Imperial Wizard of the White Knights of the Klan, had organized a group to carry out the Dahmer assignment. Bowers already was under indictment for organizing the killing of Goodman, Schwerner and Chaney, but he was not scheduled to go on trial until October 1967.

Bowers was an unusual individual. He considered himself to be highly intelligent and he had attended the University of Southern California and studied engineering. He was originally from Mississippi and established a business in Laurel that did extremely well. Bowers was single and our investigation indicated that he was a loner and had no interest in women. The Klan was his life. As our investigation revealed, many men wanted to join his Klan

90

group just to be around him. He had a deep hatred of Jews and blacks. At every speech he voiced his opinion that communists were taking over America and in every speech he talked about blacks raping white women. Klan membership grew substantially under Bowers' leadership. He played on the fears of many white people. Although the Klan was very active in burning churches, beatings, and in some cases murder, Bowers was not satisfied and he wanted to show those in Washington that the Klan in Mississippi was bigger than ever.

The *Laurel Leader*, a daily newspaper, was firebombed after printing a story that Bowers had been subpoenaed before the House Un-American Committee and had taken the Fifth and his chief lieutenant, Deavers Nix, who was described as Bowers' chief of the Klan investigative bureau, had also taken the Fifth. No one was injured in the bombing, but the Klan wanted to let the editors know that they were in charge and they did not care for the stories being written about the Klan.

Each known Klansman and suspect was assigned to an FBI agent. That agent had to determine the whereabouts of that individual on January 10, 1966, and it was up to the FBI agent to do everything possible to either have that individual as a suspect or to eliminate him completely. Jim Awe and I had several assignments on different individuals. Nix operated John's Café in downtown Laurel, where the Klansmen assembled. They were instructed that they did not have to be interviewed by the FBI because the Bureau was composed of Yankee outsiders who were in line with the communists.

The day after the murder, FBI Special Agent Jim Awe and I went to the home of a known KKK member, who lived outside the city of Laurel. As we approached the house, he appeared on the front porch, brandishing a double-barreled shotgun.

"I'm gonna shoot both of you men if you don't turn and run," he shouted.

I moved to the left, toward the protection of a tree, and Agent Awe moved to the right.

"We're with the FBI," I shouted back. "We won't turn our back on you. All we want is to talk with you about your whereabouts on the night Vernon Dahmer was killed."

"I'll tell you one more time to get off my property or I'm gonna open fire."

"If you raise the barrel of that shotgun, you should know that we are armed. You can't kill both of us. One of us will have to kill you."

The Klansman began to shake, tears streaming down his face.

"I don't want any problems. I've got orders not to be interviewed."

His wife and their three sons stood nearby, watching as he cried and begged for us to leave him alone. At about that time his brother drove up in a pickup truck. He stuck his head out the window and shouted, "Let me talk with him just a minute."

"Go ahead," we told him.

The brother took the Klansman and his family into the house. After a few minutes the brother emerged and told us that his brother would talk to us at another time at the brother's house. Then he shook his head and said, "I'm surprised my brother didn't shoot you because he's probably the meanest of the Jones County bunch."

We agreed to interview him at another time and left. The problem was not over our request for an interview, which he didn't have to do at that moment, but over his threats toward federal agents while holding a shotgun. The brother defused the problem by taking him inside the house.

After the interview, which we conducted at the brother's house, we concluded that he was not involved in Dahmer's murder. The confrontation was resolved without an arrest, but we let the Klan know that FBI agents could not be intimidated.

Still, they persisted in their resistance.

On another occasion Jim Awe and I staked out a suspect's home by parking across the street. When he emerged from his house and walked toward a car parked in his driveway, we got out of our cars and walked toward him, stating that we wanted to talk to him. We identified ourselves as FBI agents and asked if we could make arrangements to talk with him. We told him that he did not have to make any statement, but any statement he did make could be used against him in a court of law. As we were speaking, he interrupted us and said he knew he had a right to consult his attorney, but he understood he did not have to say one word if he did not want to.

We asked about his whereabouts on January 9, 1966, and the early morning of the following day.

"Now you are asking me questions, and I do not have to answer any," he said, "But if you have something you want to tell me, go ahead—you [are the ones] who want to talk."

*   *   *

As word spread quickly among the Klan that FBI agents would not be intimidated, anonymous phone calls were received at the homes of some of the agents assigned to Laurel. Bob Lee contacted the leader of the local Klavern and told him that if his wife or any other wives received any more anonymous calls from Klansmen that he was going to hold the leader responsible. Our informants told us the word passed to local Klan ranks that harassment of local agents should stop because "we've got to live with them."

The investigation was proceeding well. We were able to identify those involved in the killing of Dahmer, but we ran into difficulty after Bowers and Nix returned from Washington and Bowers explained to other Klan members that they did extremely well representing the Klan by taking the Fifth.

Roy Moore instructed Jim Awe and me to promptly interview Nix upon his return from Washington. We went to Nix's residence because we knew that if we went to his café in downtown Laurel we would be confronted not only by people dining at the café, but also by other Klansmen. So we went to Nix's residence and as we walked up to his house, Nix came outside and in a rage yelled at us: "Why are you spending so much time on that nigger when you should be investigating communism?"

He shouted for his wife to call the police. Then he told us he intended to file a formal complaint against us. Nix was told that we needed to verify his whereabouts on January 10 and again he flew into a rage and said, "I do not have to talk to you."

We agreed that he had that right, but we explained that it would be simpler if we could sit down and chat with him, either there or at his restaurant.

In just a matter of minutes, Laurel police officers in two cars arrived. Nix demanded that we be arrested for threatening him and using profane language and disturbing the peace. We told the officers that the purpose of our visit was not confrontational. We explained that all we wanted to do was to talk to him. The police were considerate, knowing that was the purpose of law enforcement. They refused any action, which further enraged Nix. Nix later filed an affidavit which was very extensive about an incident on his property on February 11, 1966. This placed the police in an unusual position.

We explained to Moore that there was an arrest warrant out for us in Jones County and that we should perhaps work in Forrest County for a while. Moore was not amused. He said that we should continue to work in Jones County and not be intimidated. To do otherwise would set the tone that the Klan, particularly in Jones County, could do exactly as it pleased.

Two other agents attempted to question the Klansman and immediately the Klansman's frustrations began to spill out. "I'm a white Anglo-Saxon protestant," he said. "I am not a Catholic, Jew or Turk. Why won't you leave me alone? We have local law to handle things here. If you amounted to anything, you would quit the FBI and get a decent job. All you listen to is Jews, Niggers and communists. Why don't you go to New York where all the niggers are raping white women?"

The agents would not leave until they received the information they wanted to gather from the individual. The FBI had learned in their investigation of the Charles Mack Parker matter in Neshoba County and in the investigation in Franklin County murder of two black teenagers, Moore and Dees, that if you allowed certain individuals to get the upper hand, then you would not be successful. We heard so many times, while covering demonstrations and marches and doing interviews: "Hey there Federal Bureau of Investigation—you're for the niggers and Jews and not the white people."

Director Hoover had confided in Governor Johnson that agents had been spat upon, received harassing calls at their home, found rattlesnakes inside their cars, and that he had ordered the agents to take control of the situation. Had the FBI not challenged the Klan, we believe there would have been a total breakdown of law enforcement.

Governor Johnson was very receptive to the agents conducting the investigation and setting up a command post in Hattiesburg because that was his home. He was from Forrest County and he knew that the Klan would take control if allowed to do so. It is noted that Hattiesburg is also the home of the University of Southern Mississippi and all during the times that we had marches, demonstrations and Klan rallies, the students were never involved. They were in school during those months, but they chose not to get involved. We were very pleased because we knew what had happened at Ole Miss three years prior, which ended up being a sad situation.

SAC Moore also had been sending Gov. Johnson letters on a confidential basis setting forth what we knew about the Klan membership. I know from my supervision of work at that time that a letter was sent on August 20, 1964, and another letter was sent on September 23, 1965, which was hand-delivered to the governor, setting out the names of those individuals in law enforcement that were members of the Klan. The list included sheriff's deputies, Mississippi highway patrol officers, judges, and constables. We also sent a list of known Klansmen in different Klaverns across the state, which Governor Johnson acknowledged was important to have in his possession.

The investigation went extremely well in the Dahmer murder, and we were pleased that we were proceeding at a rapid pace. We conducted an investigation of several people outside of the state. In fact Thompson Webb and I drove to Georgia one night to interview Mr. Dahmer's sons, who were in the military, to get some answers that we needed at that time. That's what made it sad. The Dahmer family was loved in the community and their sons were all in the military serving their country while the Klan was killing their father.

A weapon that we found at the scene was eventually traced to Roy Pitts and out of that we were able to charge eleven men in a federal conspiracy. However, the trial ended with a hung jury on April 29, 1969. It was left to the State of Mississippi to try the defendants and each had to be tried separately on murder and arson charges. One of the eleven was Sam Bowers. A search of his home in Laurel revealed a large cache of firearms and other weapons.

This was an unusual case as it involved a rising young business leader who had been honored in Laurel for his business ventures, Charles Clifford Wilson. The others were William Thomas Smith, Cecil Sessum, Billy Ray Pitts, Lester Thornton, Henry Deboxtil, Charles Noble, Frank Lyons, Deveaurix Nix, and Travis Gills. It is noted that Wilson was sentenced later in state court; Smith, Sessum, and Pitts plead guilty and became key witnesses. Thornton was never tried. Deboxtil, Noble, and Lyons all ended in mistrial. Nix and Gills were never tried.

In 1998, the State of Mississippi decided to bring Sam Bowers to trial and District Attorney Lindsay Car, backed by Mississippi Attorney General Mike Moore, reopened the case against Bowers. The state's case was skillfully presented by Bob Helfrich of the Forrest County district attorney's office and Lee Martin of the attorney general's office.

Bowers previously had served time in prison in the MIBURN case after being convicted in 1967. District Attorney Helfrich discussed with me the procedures for the trial because in 1998 I was commissioner of public safety managing the highway patrol. After reviewing the work done in 1966, the DA subpoenaed Loren Brooks, Jim Awe, Charles Killion and me to testify against Bowers.

Prior to the trial, I accidently met Bowers in the courthouse witness room, where I had gone to get a cup of coffee. Bowers looked at me with a weird smile and said, "Well, we meet again. I know things are going to work out well."

He had on a Mickey Mouse tie, Mickey Mouse belt, and there were always rumors about him, but why he became a Mickey Mouse enthusiast no one ever knew.[1]

I said, "Yes, and I hope you are doing well."

He just stared at me without saying another word.

Although he was reported to be extremely intelligent, it did not show because Travis Buckley represented him in the Schwerner, Goodman, and Chaney matter and everyone knew that he handled Klan matters for Bowers. Again, he had Travis Buckley in 1998. Many people present contended that Buckley had passed his prime.

On August 21, 1998, the former Klan leader, who was then 73 years of age, was convicted in Hattiesburg in district court for ordering the firebombing death of Dahmer. The verdict carried an automatic life term and he was immediately sentenced by Judge

---

[1] This got the attention of co-author Dickerson, co-author of "How to Screen Adoptive and Foster Parents," a social work text for professionals that points out that neckties with cartoon characters often are used by pedophiles to attract children. They also are used by mental health professionals to establish a rapport with children.

McKenzie. This conviction marked a decisive legal battle that included the early trials in the 1960s which ended in deadlocked juries. Bowers once boasted that "no jury in the state of Mississippi is going to convict a white man for killing someone black."

The prosecuting attorney and Sheriff Billy McGee in Forrest County were outstanding in their handling of the Dahmer matter through the years. So many people deserve credit for bringing this horrendous crime to a final end. Deveaurix Nix, who was Sam Bowers' chief, was scheduled for trial after Bowers, but he died on September 12, 1998. Bowers died in prison.

The main witness in the Dahmer case was Billy Ray Pitts and he pleaded guilty, became a government witness and was placed under the protection of the government. Pitts suffered because it was his pistol that was dropped at the crime scene. Even though the serial numbers had almost been erased it took the FBI a long time to fully get all the facts and previous owners of the gun. We were able to convince Pitts that his best bet was to proceed as a government witness. Pitts later was convinced by his brother, a minister in Los Angeles, to testify and he publicly apologized to the Dahmer family for his actions and said the only reason he agreed to testify was to give closure to the Dahmer family.

* * *

On January 14, 1966, James Seale, the primary suspect in the Moore and Dee murders, appeared before the House Committee on Un-American Activities in Washington, D.C. Chomping down on a cigar, he refused to answer over forty questions, citing his Fifth Amendment rights. In some circles, he was quite the hero. After the state closed its files on the murder case, the news media lost interest in Seale. He had every reason to think that it would be clear sailing from that point on. He had beaten the system.

A free man, Seale pursued the American Dream. He flew crop dusters all across Mississippi and Louisiana, living the good life. At that time, crop duster pilots were viewed as romantic figures who defied death at every turn. By the 1970s, he'd also found work as a police officer in Vidalia, Louisiana. In his off-hours, he continued to chase boll weevils from the air and took paying riders up in his plane so that they could see the majesty of the Mississippi River from the air. He was slowed somewhat in 1970, when his plane collided with another airplane, resulting in the deaths of five people. Seale escaped unscathed.

Two years later, he drove his crop duster into a soybean field, suffering cuts and bruises, and a broken wrist. By the 1980s, Seale had returned to Franklin County, where he lived a quiet life, so quiet that most people in the community assumed that he was dead.

7

MISSISSIPPI JEWS IN THE CROSSHAIRS

On September 18, 1967, the sullen stillness of a summery night was shattered in Jackson, Mississippi, by an explosion at the newly built Beth Israel synagogue, located in an affluent section of the city. Thankfully no one was at the temple because it was late at night. No one was injured or killed. I did not live too far from the synagogue, so I heard the explosion.

As head of the violent crimes desk, I rushed to the scene after awakening other agents to send them there to gather evidence. Most of the temple was destroyed by the blast and it was obvious that the damage had been done by a bomb. We spent the remainder of the night with the Jackson police, wading through debris, much of it soaked by water caused by broken pipes, looking for clues that might help us piece together a case.

An extensive investigation was conducted to identify the bombers, but we already had a good idea of who was responsible. At that time the Klan had one of the best bomb makers in the country living in the metro area of Jackson. We immediately sent agents to the homes of known Klansmen and contacted our informants in an effort to gather information.

There was no question about why the temple had been bombed. After decades of keeping a low profile, while excelling in business, medicine and law, Mississippi Jews entered a new era in 1954 with the arrival of Canadian-born rabbi Perry Nussbaum who came to Mississippi to serve the Beth Israel Congregation in Jackson. At the age of forty-six, he was a veteran of service in Australia, Massachusetts, New York, New Jersey, Kansas and Texas. Despite his extensive experience he was totally unprepared for the racial repression that he found in Mississippi.

Shortly after his arrival he was informed by leading members of the congregation that they did not want him to attract a lot of attention to the Jewish community, nor did they want him to implement new rituals to their ceremonies. In other words, they liked things just the way they were and they wanted him to follow tradition and not blaze new trails.

However, that wasn't what Nussbaum had in mind for his congregation. He felt called to be a leader, not a follower. He was committed to the Jewish concept of *tikkun olam*, greater justice. Against the advice of congregation spokespersons, he worked with black religious leaders in the community and began interfaith services that socially and racially integrated the temple. When Freedom Riders started coming to Jackson in 1961, he visited them in jail and welcomed them into his home once they were released. Individual members of his congregation pleaded with him to back away from his involvement with the Freedom Riders, but he steadfastly refused, citing a higher responsibility.

When the temple was splintered into thousands of tiny pieces by the bomb, Mississippi Jews did not scratch their heads in confusion. They knew *exactly* who was responsible for the blast—and why. They just didn't know the individuals' names.

We were in the midst of our investigation of the temple bombing when a second explosion occurred two months later at Nussbaum's home. This time the goal was murder since the rabbi and his wife were home at the time. After the blast, they stumbled from the house onto the lawn with glass fragments in their hair, stunned by the violence of the blast.

I received a call at home from Kenneth Dean, the executive director of the Mississippi Council on Human Relations, a white minister who had come to Mississippi to assist in racial reconciliation. Moments after Ken notified me of the bombing the Jackson FBI office called. I immediately rushed to the scene and joined the agents I had aroused from sleep and sent to the Nussbaum home. After a quick assessment, the other agents fanned out in search of known Klansmen and informants.

I remained behind to interview Rabbi Nussbaum, whom I had gotten to know pretty well. While we were talking, Mississippi Governor Paul Johnson and a delegation of white clergy arrived and offered their encouragement to the Nussbaums. I was standing next to the rabbi, along with Kenneth Dean, when the rabbi began to verbally attack some of the clergymen, shouting that they were the reason for the attacks since they had not spoken out about the Klan and others who were committing violent acts in the state.

The rabbi said that as far as he was concerned they were still staunch segregationists. He singled out the minister of the largest church in Mississippi, the First Baptist Church, telling him that he was fearful of being involved in any interfaith church work, fearful of being involved in any demonstrations, and fearful of being involved in voter registration. He questioned whether any of these churches were going to turn around and, as he put it, "stop putting up with this violence."

The clergymen did not stay at the scene very long after the rabbi's outburst. However, later they held a small demonstration lead by an inter-faith group, composed of whites and blacks, and marched to the synagogue. Some, but not many, of the white clergy did step forward.

The attacks came only three weeks before KKK Imperial Wizard Sam Bowers and others went on trial in federal court on charges related to the Philadelphia killings of Goodman, Schwerner and Chaney. Bowers was an ego maniac. Some described him as a lunatic. He gave the order to kill, maim and destroy the houses of worship.

It is very difficult in bombing cases where you have a building almost destroyed, breaking water pipes, and destroying possible evidence, to find enough evidence on the scene to identify those responsible. There was never sufficient evidence for prosecution, although we determined who bombed both places.

After the two bombings I suggested to Rabbi Nussbaum that it would be wise if he and his wife considered leaving the state. I was fearful for their safety. He left for a short time and then returned to Jackson, where he remained until his retirement in 1973. He died in 1987.

*   *   *

There were several confrontations between agents and Klansmen in the aftermath of those two bombings. When you try to pinpoint the time frame of a possible suspect, heated confrontations boil to the surface. We were fortunate that no agents were killed in the 1960s because the threat was always there.

In the months after the bombing of Beth Israel, we also had a bombing of the synagogue in Meridian. Bear in mind, the Jewish community was great to work with and they wanted to do everything possible to ensure the safety of their families, their homes, and their lifestyle. As a result many in the Jewish community began to carry guns. Al Binder, a local attorney and businessman Joe Harris and others worked diligently behind the scenes to assist the FBI, and they made funds available, if needed, to develop informants in an effort to solve some of the attacks.

In the months after the bombing of Beth Israel and the temple in Meridian, Myer Davidson, a Jewish businessman in Meridian, attracted the attention of the Klan when he said publicly that the bombings that occurred were an attack on all Jews. As a result, Sam Bowers targeted Myer Davidson and we know by evidence that Bowers ordered the bombings of the Davidson home on June 29, 1968. FBI agents Jack Rucker and Frank Watts had been working with Chief Gunn of the Meridian Police Department for quite some time and there was mutual respect between Chief Gunn and the agents.

The FBI in Mississippi, specifically Roy Moore and I, advised the Jewish leaders that to stave off attacks we needed to get more informants inside the Klan and it would take money. We needed to know if there were other attacks planned on Jewish businessmen, as well as attacks planned on the targeted Davidson. The Jewish community raised almost $100,000 for that purpose.

It was then up to the FBI to deliver. These were difficult times. Riots had occurred in major cities across the country—Los Angeles, Detroit, Chicago, and others—and there was so much lawlessness going on around the country that the FBI was stressed to come up with informants with good intelligence to stave off these attacks. Everything seemed to be exploding nationwide and Mississippi and was not an exception.

Jack Rucker and Frank Watts, two outstanding agents assigned to the Meridian office of the FBI, had been instrumental in working against the Klan. And they began to develop additional informants. Attorney Tom Hendricks, a former FBI agent who had been involved in the Mississippi Burning case because he was the attorney for Bernard Akin, was approached by Watts and Rucker to help them with the Roberts brothers, Alton Wayne and Raymond. Hendricks had been successful in getting an acquittal for Akin and was looked upon by some Klan members as a good man because, in his cross examination in the Mississippi Burning case, he drew raves for his defense of Akin (Akins died in 1968). Hendricks had the respect of the Roberts brothers because of his previous work on behalf of the Klan.

102

Hendricks approached the Roberts and said he knew they were being contacted by Watts and Rucker and he wanted to help in the negotiation. Hendricks also knew that the Jewish community in Mississippi had donated a large sum of money and he made it clear that he wanted part of the money.

Hendricks drove the Roberts brothers to Agent Watts' home in the middle of the night and they had a heart-to-heart. They knew the Roberts would know if anything was planned in Meridian, Mississippi. In dealing with the Roberts, the agents had to be very careful, as they remained vicious. Alton Wayne had already been convicted in federal court on civil rights violations in killing Schwerner and Goodman. He was the shooter.

Alton Wayne thought he might get some help with his conviction. He was out on appeal waiting to serve a 10-year sentence. Alton Wayne was told that there was no way he could get help in that regard. His sentence was set in stone. He would have to serve his time. But he was informed that here was some big-time money available if they would cooperate in identifying those responsible for the bombing of the synagogues as well as any future attacks on Jewish businesses or members of the Jewish community. The Roberts agreed to further meetings.

The Meridian police department had already assigned their top people to work with Roberts and the FBI. The police in Meridian, as well as the FBI, kept pressure on the Roberts because they knew that anything that might happen in the Meridian area would involve the Roberts.

After other meetings with the Roberts brothers and Hendricks, Alton Wayne identified Thomas Albert Tarrants III as the individual who intended to bomb the Davidson home. Twenty-one years of age, he stood six feet three and weighed 170 pounds. The son of a used car salesman, he was a native of Alabama, where he attended Murphy High School in Mobile and protested the admission of blacks to the school. By the age of seventeen, he had dabbled in various right-wing organizations including the National States Rights Party, the Minutemen, and the Ku Klux Klan. His racist obsessions were not confined to a hatred of blacks. He also hated Jews, whom he believed enabled blacks to win civil rights victories in the South.

One year before the Roberts brothers fingered Tarrants as a potential bomber, he had boldly knocked on the door of Sam Bowers' pin-ball machine company in Laurel, Mississippi, and introduced himself to the Imperial Wizard of the White Knights of the Ku Klux Klan. He told Bowers he had travelled from Alabama to obtain a job at the Masonite Corporation plant, which was located across the road from the rundown building that housed Bower's business. He presented himself more or less as a professional terrorist who, despite his young age, was willing to undertake any mission to drive a nail into the coffin of the so-called Jewish-black conspiracy.

Tarrants got off to a good start with Bowers by ranting about how the Jews were ruining everything in Mississippi for white people. That was the kind of talk that caught Bowers' attention. He considered himself a scholar of sorts and he had long been perturbed by his fellow Klansmen's inability to intellectually grasp the Jewish threat. As a result, he befriended the Alabama refugee and they met in secret locations so as not to attract attention. For his part, Tarrants got a job at Masonite as a maintenance worker and tried to blend into the community. Together he and Bowers plotted the bombing murder of Jewish Meridian businessman Meyer Davidson and his wife, Frances. He was targeted because of his success and influence in the community. He and his brothers built their father's junk business into the Southern Pipe Company, a major distributor of plumbing supplies.

The Roberts brothers told us the attack would occur on June 27. We reported that to Police Chief Roy Gunn and he asked Davidson and his wife to leave the house for the night. They did, although reluctantly. When the attack did not occur Davidson was highly irritated that it was a false alarm.

Then we were told that the attack would be on June 29. This time Davidson resisted leaving his house, proclaiming that he had work to do and had no time for such foolishness.

In working with Davidson it was necessary for him to move his family away from the residence and not create any suspicion from the neighbors, except ones that he truly wanted to rely upon. After much debate, he agreed to leave his house and check into a motel, but only on the condition that his favorite chair would be loaded into the car and taken to the motel.

Once Davidson left with his chair, police officers and FBI agents armed with shotguns, pistols and rifles, encircled the house. Some crouched behind bushes. Others stood behind trees. Others took up positions on the embankment across the street from the house. FBI agents Frank Watts and Jack Rucker persuaded Chief Gunn to leave the scene, fearing he would be an emotional loose cannon during the operation. He had good reason to be emotional. The Klan had threatened both him and his family with violence.

Watts and Rucker evacuated the house directly across from the Davidson home, and took up positions at a bedroom window.

With everyone in place—and the house darkened—police and FBI agents waited.

* * *

Tarrants began his death mission in Jackson, where he picked up his girlfriend—and partner in crime—Kathy Ainsworth, whom he had met in Mobile, Alabama. Ainsworth, 26-years-of age, was a fifth-grade teacher at Lorena Duling Elementary School, where she had fooled parents, teachers and students into thinking that her highest priority in life was to provide a loving, quality education to the children entrusted in her care. Unknown to those who had daily contact with her, Ainsworth led a secret life. Not only was she romantically involved with Tarrants, she shared his extremist views about blacks and Jews. In short, she was a terrorist.

After picking her up, Tarrants drove Ainsworth to a restaurant just outside the city on the banks of the Ross Barnett Reservoir, a large body of water that serves as the primary water supply for the City of Jackson and surrounding communities. It was named for former Governor Barnett, who was best known for attempting to block the racial integration of the University of Mississippi. To Tarrants and Ainsworth, Barnett was a heroic figure. It was fitting that they had their potential last supper at his shrine.

After dinner, Tarrants and Ainsworth set out for Meridian, a drive of about 80 miles. In the trunk of Tarrants's rickety green Buick were their chosen implements of murder—a box of dynamite, along with two machine guns, and several hand grenades. As they drove through the night to their destiny, police and FBI agents, wearing black T-shirts and dark trousers, hunkered down in the shadows and waited for their arrival. Before long authorities saw the green Buick approach the Davidson home and pull over to the curb. There was a second person in the car, but they could not clearly see who it was. They had no intelligence on a second person.

Tarrants got out of the car with the bomb cradled under his left arm, and an automatic pistol in his right hand. He began walking slowly toward the Davidson home. Suddenly, the stillness of the night air was broken by the sound of a human voice—"Halt! Police!"

Hearing that, Tarrants turned and fired his weapon, drawing the fire of the police officers. Then he dropped his gun and the bomb and raced to the car, zigzagging like a running back avoiding tacklers. By the time he reached the car, a load of buckshot had torn into his upper right leg.

Everyone, it seemed, let loose with everything they had, sending buckshot and bullets into the Buick. Tarrants's partner reached over and opened the driver's door for him, catching two loads of buckshot in her shoulder. She cried out that she was hit. Just moments later she took a rifle slug through her neck, severing her spine. Now Tarrants and his partner were both shot.

Despite his wounds, Tarrants was able to speed away with police attempting to stop him. Two Meridian police officers, Mike Hatcher and Tom Tucker, chased after them in pursuit. Finally, after a high-speed chase, they were able to ram Tarrants's car, forcing him to crash. Tarrants jumped out of the car, spraying officers with machine gun fire. He attempted to scale an electrified fence, but he was knocked down by the electrical current.

During the shootout, Hatcher was seriously wounded. Tucker's shots hit Tarrants and he dropped his weapon. By then other police officers arrived and secured the arrest of Tarrants. During the shootout, a U.S. sailor, who lived nearby, ran out into his yard to see what was going on and where the shooting was coming from. The sailor was caught in the crossfire and was wounded. Medical personnel arrived at the scene and transported the wounded sailor and Hatcher to the hospital. After being identified, Tarrants was transported by ambulance to the hospital with an FBI agent who was sent to travel with him in the event he tried to escape, although he was very seriously wounded and at that time not expected to live. Throughout it all, Tarrants never made any statements to law enforcement officers.

Hatcher was immediately flown to Atlanta for surgery since he was in critical condition. Fortunately, he survived. He is a most unusual individual. As a member of the Meridian police department, he became a member of the Klan and later testified in the trial of Bowers and others in Meridian in 1967. As a Klansman, Hatcher met with Edgar Ray Killen the day after the disappearance of Goodman, Schwerner and Chaney and was told the details of the killings.

When the police looked inside the Buick they discovered the body of Kathy Ainsworth. She was wearing shorts and a tank top, all covered with blood. The FBI immediately started searching records for information about her. I vividly recall that, despite what the news media reported in some circles, we had no prior knowledge of the activities of Kathy Ainsworth.

An examination of Ainsworth's young life revealed that she, like Tarrants, was from Mobile. They had met and spent a lot of time together while in Mobile. Kathy's maiden name was Capomacchia. She was raised in Miami and her family later moved to Mobile. Kathy attended Mississippi College, a Baptist-affiliated institution located in Clinton, a suburb of Jackson. She married Ralph Ainsworth and they resided in Jackson.

Kathy, an attractive brunette, was described as a quiet and extremely kind person who worked well with teachers and her young students. Only a handful of Klansmen knew that she was a teacher by day and a terrorist by night. After the shoot out in Meridian, an informant advised us that Bowers was livid and "all hell broke out." Tarrants was like a son to Bowers and he immediately hired an attorney to visit with Tarrants and represent him. Bowers also wanted to know who had tipped off the FBI and police about Tarrants's plans.

Many Klan members across the state were tight-lipped and realized that their group had been infiltrated to the point that they wanted no further part of the Klan. Many Klan members refused to attend Klan meetings. The effect was immediate. After the shooting of Tarrants, and the killing of Ainsworth, the violence ceased in Mississippi. With Tarrants recovering from his wounds and in jail awaiting trial, other Klan members were so skittish that they did not trust each other. Many of the wives, according to informants, begged their husbands to drop out of the Klan. The

Roberts brothers were paid for information with a large amount of money that had been gathered by the Jewish community.

Bowers still attacked the Jewish community as he and his close associates scrutinized everyone around them to determine who had betrayed them. Tarrants also was interested in who betrayed him. He informed agents Watts and Rucker that he would help them if they would disclose the informant that betrayed him. Tarrants went on trial in Meridian on November 25, 1968, and after a short two-day trail, he was found guilty and the judge sentenced him to 30 years in the state penitentiary at Parchman.

Upon arrival at the state prison, located in the flat Delta area of Mississippi, Tarrants began to search for ways to escape. Very few people, during my career, were able to escape from Parchman. They were usually caught in a short length of time by tracking dogs and they were easily spotted as they ran across the flat Delta farmland. Despite the challenges, Tarrants was able to escape in July 1969 with two other prisoners, thanks to the efforts of others from the inside and outside. A car was provided and a place to hold up for several days was provided to them in a wooded area in rural Rankin County near Jackson.

Tarrants was given food, equipment, and weapons by Klan members so that they would be able to live for many days before moving on to another state. The FBI had so infiltrated the Klan by that point that we knew almost every move that they made. An informant told us where the three escapees were hiding out. The FBI and the highway patrol devised a plan whereby J. D. Gardner, chief of the highway patrol, and myself would survey the area in a helicopter to determine if we could stop the escapees. Our agents and the state police took a position in an area across the Pearl River in a location where we hoped to drive the escapees.

This was a difficult mission in some respects. The pilot, a fellow by the name of George, weighed 275 pounds; Gardner weighed about 220 pounds; and I weighed around 230 pounds. We got into this two-seater helicopter, the small bubble type, to make the survey. I was seated to the right, J. D. was in the middle and the pilot was on the left at the controls.

Every time we made a circle, and the helicopter swung to the right, the weight of those two men pressed against me. Finally, I yelled out, "I'm going to fall out of this thing."

The pilot responded, "Don't worry chief, the door handle on that thing is broken and it's not supposed to come open."

That was not the information I wanted to hear.

Finally, we spotted the camp where the escapees were holed up. They were encamped near the Jackson Municipal Airport and planes were taking off and landing and helicopters were taking off and landing. We immediately landed at the airport and went to the scene to move in on the escapees.

Rex Armistead was the chief investigator for the highway patrol and he was armed with his own machinegun and ready for action. As we moved in, we used a bullhorn to encourage Tarrants and the other escapees to surrender. We pointed out that they had no means of escape and should come out with their hands up.

One of the escapees, a convicted bank robber from Indianapolis, immediately opened fire on the police officers, prompting a burst of fire from the FBI agents and Mississippi Highway Patrol. Rex Armistead opened up with his machinegun and just about everyone had to duck as every small pine tree in his way was cut down. The gunfire continued for several minutes, after which there was total silence.

Finally, Tarrants shouted, "We give up, we give up!"

As officers moved in and took Tarrants and one of the other escapees into custody, the bank robber was found crumpled, with his head completely blown away. Tarrants I'm sure, after looking at his dead partner, knew that he had suffered enough the year before and would definitely be killed this time.

Tarrants and the other escapee were transported back to Parchman and interviewed in depth about how they escaped. Once again there was an immediate ripple effect as the Klan saw that whatever they did someone was going to be telling the FBI and the police on them. Many of them had escaped going to prison, but they knew the time had come that they should cease their violent activities. Tarrants, of course, ended up having a very happy ending because Watts continued in his belief that Tarrants could help resolve other crimes.

Watts traveled to Parchman to visit Tarrants, as did Ken Dean in his minister's role, and they played a major role in convincing Tarrants to give up his violent ways. Between Watts and Ken Dean, Tarrants changed his life. When he eventually was paroled, he married a wonderful lady, a lady of means, and they are currently living a good life together. I will not disclose the area where they currently live or what he does as I think he would want to keep his life private after a life of terrorism.

* * *

During the time that Jews were under attack in Mississippi, many members of the black community wanted to take action against the Klan. Several marches were held in Forrest County, calling for immediate action, as the black community was sick and tired of being killed, beaten and having crosses burned at their residences and their churches. It was an explosive situation, but Mr. Charles Evers, who had assumed a leadership role since the death of his brother, Medgar, was able to convince them that the FBI should be allowed to do its work.

8

MARTIN LUTHER KING ASSASSINATION

On November 18, 1964, FBI Director J. Edgar Hoover invited eighteen women reporters to his office for coffee. Over the course of a three-hour "interview," Hoover condemned the violence taking place in Mississippi, saying that "in the southern part of the state, in the swamp country, the only inhabitants seem to be rattlesnakes, water moccasins, and redneck sheriffs."

It was not until Hoover was asked about Martin Luther King's criticism of the FBI for not assigning non-Southern agents to the FBI satellite office in Albany, Georgia, that he got into trouble. Martin Luther King, he boldly proclaimed, was "the most notorious liar in the country." The repercussions of that comment sent ripples all the way to Jackson.

To my way of thinking, if you work for a man, you've got to be loyal to that man, and I certainly was loyal to Mr. Hoover. When he called King a notorious liar, his words went all over the world. Of course, many officials in Washington, including the president, were very upset at the time. It certainly appeared that Mr. Hoover might be leaving as director after making those statements.

The FBI did not need that fight because you had FBI agents that had to know what was going on in the black community. We had Stokley Carmichael coming into Mississippi with a propensity for violence and it made it difficult for FBI agents such as myself who were trying to find black informants. We had many in the black community who wanted to help us, but after that statement by Mr. Hoover, many of the prominent blacks just did not want to have anything to do with the FBI.

I had one of the best black informants in Mississippi that we counted upon and Mr. Hoover's comments created a hell of a mess for us, trying to convince members of the black community that we were their friends when our boss was castigating Dr. King. It was not good, but we had to bite our tongue. It made it very difficult for the FBI in the South. Lyndon Johnson was the president and he said, "I'd rather have Hoover on the inside pissing out than on the outside pissing in." Many in the black community still do not trust the FBI because of the treatment of Dr. King by Mr. Hoover.

In 1967 there were riots across the country. In July race riots broke out in Cleveland, Flint, South Bend and Phoenix. Dr. King made public appeals for the rioting to end, reminding his followers that he was an advocate of non-violence. That same month rioting broke out in Detroit, prompting the U.S. Army to send in the 82nd Airborne Division to help restore order.

In an attempt to counter Dr. King's non-violence influence, activists such as Stokley Carmichael and H. Rap Brown called for a revolution. As the year wore on, white students opposed to the war in Vietnam joined in with black protesters. In the evening, it was rare to turn on television and not see coverage of massive street demonstrations.

In March 1968, Dr. King and his staff traveled to Memphis to support a strike called by the city's sanitation workers. He returned a week later and marched through the streets of Memphis with about 5,000 demonstrators. Unfortunately, violence broke out when the marchers reached Main Street, resulting in extensive looting, the shooting of four marchers, and the arrests of over three hundred demonstrators.

Dr. King returned to Atlanta and weighed his options. If he did not return to Memphis and take control of the situation, his message of non-violence could lose ground to the black leaders who were calling for violent revolution. On April 3, 1968, Dr. King and his staff arrived in Memphis and drove to the Lorraine Motel, checking in around noon.

That night he addressed a crowd of about 12,000 at the Mason Temple, telling the audience, "It really doesn't matter with me now, because I've been to the mountain top." The following day, April 4, Dr. King and his staff remained all day at the Lorraine Motel. At 6:01 p.m. Dr. King stepped out on the balcony for a breath of fresh air. His driver, Solomon Jones, shouted up at him that he needed his overcoat. It was a chilly fifty-five degrees.

"OK, I will," Dr. King responded.

It was at that moment that a shot rang out.

A .30-06-caliber bullet ripped into his neck and jaw, dropping him to the concrete floor. He was rushed to St. Joseph's Hospital, where he was pronounced dead within thirty minutes of his arrival. With his death, the FBI began one of the largest manhunts in its history, looking for the individual or individuals who had assassinated Dr. King.

I was in the Jackson field office at the time. I received the telephone call from the Memphis FBI office informing us that Dr. King had been shot. We immediately put our plan into action to locate and interview individuals who were suspected of violence. After conferring with Mr. Moore, the Jackson SAC, an order went out that every agent across Mississippi had to locate those individuals assigned to that agent, and eyeball each one, and then make sure that individual had not been in Memphis around 6 p.m.

This scramble resulted in a few incidents with Klansmen who did not want to be interviewed and did not want to tell the FBI of their whereabouts. Several were unaware of the assassination and when told by agents they did not mind cooperating. If an individual was at work, we went to the workplace. If he happened to be out during the evening at a particular nightspot, he had to be confronted. We knew there was always a possibility that the person or persons who assassinated Dr King would have to travel in Mississippi.

We had every agent in Mississippi knocking on doors. We wanted that agent to be able to come back and say, "I went to his house, got him out of bed or interrupted his dinner, and he was there at 6 o'clock." If the suspect was working the night shift, they had to go to his place of work and actually see him on the job. Then we would go down the list and say these are the individuals that we know could not have been in Memphis and these are the individuals we couldn't find.

One of the first people that I suspected was J. B. Stoner, the Georgia segregationist who was the long-time chairman of the National States' Rights Party, the political arm of the KKK. As it turned out, Stoner was speaking in Meridian at the time of the murder. Our agents were across the street in a building with the lights off monitoring what was going on. All of a sudden they heard cheering and clapping. The people in the audience had just gotten word on the radio that King had been assassinated. They ended up pouring out into the streets, jumping up and down to celebrate his death. At least the agents knew where J. B. Stoner was that night.

Mourners view the body of Martin Luther King Jr. in 1968. Photo courtesy of the Mississippi Valley Collection, University of Memphis, University Libraries

Through the years, Klan leader Sam Bowers and others had put out word that if Dr. King ever came to Mississippi, there would be a bounty to kill him. Aware of that possibility, Dr. King only traveled to Mississippi when it was necessary, such as when he went to Philadelphia after the Goodman, Schwerner and Chaney murders. The FBI and the highway patrol were there. So was I. Dr. King made a statement in Philadelphia that it was the meanest looking crowd he'd ever encountered. It was difficult for the patrol and local authorities to keep order during this small march. We were all pleased when Dr. King left Mississippi because we always were concerned that someone would attempt to kill him.

Many pages have been written about the life of Dr. King and his assassination by James Earl Ray, a petty thief and small-time crook, who wanted his fifteen minutes of fame. Whether he was ever paid to assassinate Dr. King has never been legitimately determined. Based upon an exhaustive investigation, the findings of the select committee on the assassination of Dr. King revealed that one shot killed Dr. King and Ray fired that shot.

The shot that killed Dr. King was fired from a bathroom window of a rooming house in the 400 block of South Main Street in Memphis. Ray purchased the rifle, which he dropped on the street after the shooting, and fled the scene after the assassination. He ended up in London, where he was arrested by two burly FBI agents who had been dispatched to London to return Ray to the United States. I knew both of these agents. They were assigned to the firearms unit at the training academy at Quantico and they were perfect to send to London to escort Ray back to the United States.

Andrew Young and the family of Dr. King, including Coretta Scott King, were never convinced that Ray was the lone gunman. The sad part is that Ray pleaded guilty and died in prison before all questions could be addressed. Many in the black community heard rumors through the years of a conspiracy, but there is no substantial evidence to prove that a conspiracy existed. In all the records that I personally reviewed, including Klan records that contained information that certain individuals wanted to lure King to Mississippi to be assassinated, the conspiracy rumors just never held up.

When the world received the information that Dr. King had been assassinated, several major cities erupted in riots. It was a sad day, where you had people breaking into stores, stealing, burning and looting. It took a long time to recover. After that, the FBI had a difficult time getting good intelligence from certain segments of the black community.

When Mr. Hoover allowed Assistant Director Bill Sullivan to mail certain audio tapes to selected news media and also to Coretta Scott King, setting out some of the personal activities of Dr. King, this also did not help the working agents in the field. These so-called sex tapes were harmful because there was a certain element of individuals who delighted in these revelations.

At the same time, there was another element that did not approve of the disclosure of the tapes. U.S. Attorney General Bobby Kennedy had approved some of the wiretaps and President Kennedy was aware of them. Certainly President Lyndon Johnson listened to the tapes provided by the FBI. The original wiretaps were designed to see what Communists might be involved with Dr. King—and if he happened to be receiving any funds from Communist sympathizers.

Instead, the tapes mainly brought out the affairs of Dr. King. This did not work well for the agents working in the field who had to obtain intelligence on the violence-prone individuals in the U.S., especially the Black Panthers, who were creating havoc from coast to coast, because you had non-violent leaders in the black community who were so disturbed over the wiretaps that they did not feel like they could trust the FBI.

* * *

As I look back on the 1960s, I remember vividly the march led by Dr. Martin Luther King in Philadelphia in 1965, one year after the disappearance of the three civil rights workers near that city. King came to Mississippi to participate in memorial services for the slain men.

As King and about 250 demonstrators marched toward the courthouse, a mob gathered around him and several trucks turned into the crowd, knocking a young boy to the ground. Some individuals in the mob tossed large firecrackers called cherry bombs into the crowd, creating panic among the demonstrators. Fistfights erupted and quickly evaporated like summer storms. Faced with potential chaos, King withdrew and returned three days later to complete the memorial services, this time without incident.

116

In a report by Jackson Special Agent in Charge Roy Moore, our difficult situation was described in detail: "These agents reported their observations to Special Agent Proctor, who relayed them directly to the Jackson office by telephone, from his observation post. The agents exposed themselves to certain dangers in order to obtain an on-the-scene account of the situation and to observe any incidents that might have taken place. They were able to affect liaison with both Negro and law enforcement officials, thereby being in a position to give a minute to minute report on the situation. Agents also made every effort to identify the perpetrators of any acts of violence they observed . . . [with] the operation of an office on a 24-hour basis in Philadelphia, these agents did an outstanding job working long hours and asking no quarter."

King subsequently confided to friends that he'd feared for his life that day in Philadelphia more than at any other time in his life. I am not surprised. I was there to see it. It is not the sort of thing one forgets.

Jim Ingram in Washington office with FBI Director Clarence M. Kelley

9

UNDER THE LOOKING GLASS

Mississippi was in turmoil in 1970, as was most of the country, over the United States military invasion of Cambodia. On May 4, Ohio National Guardsmen were called to Kent State College during a student protest over the invasion and the Vietnam War in general. The guardsmen, for reasons never fully explained, opened fire on the students, killing four and wounding nine others, some of whom were walking to class and not involved in the protest.

After the incident, passions ran high. In a letter to my co-author in 1970, Doris Krause, the grief-stricken mother of Allison Krause, one of the students killed by guardsmen, expressed her grief over the loss of her daughter, writing, "I do not recognize the world any longer; it has changed beyond all nightmares."

It was a sentiment that we all could share.

FBI Inspector Joe Sullivan was called in to head up an investigation at Kent State. Ten days later, a protest erupted at Jackson State University over the Kent State killings and the wars in Cambodia and Vietnam. At the heart of the protests were concerns over escalating call-ups of eighteen and nineteen year olds to fight the unpopular war. In response, Mississippi Governor John Bell Williams ordered the National Guard to mobilize at the campus. However, before the guardsmen arrived, the governor ordered the highway patrol to the campus, where they combined forces with dozens of Jackson policemen.

Leading the force of highway patrolmen and city police officers was a twenty-three-foot-long armored vehicle that had been nicknamed Thompson's Tank (after a Jackson mayor). Ten men armed with Thompson sub-machine guns and shotguns crouched inside the tank. Two enormous spotlights were perched on the roof of the tank. As the tank moved through the campus, surrounded by a large force of officers with shotguns, the intimidating spotlights were directed onto the buildings and into the dormitories.

At one point the tank stopped and a man in a white shirt addressed students with a bullhorn. As he spoke, a bottle flew from a window and shattered on the street with a loud pop, prompting the police officers to open fire with machine guns and shotguns, spraying the walls and windows with gunfire. Two students were killed and twelve were wounded.

U.S. Attorney General John Mitchell, who had recently taken office, ordered J. Edgar Hoover to send additional FBI agents to Mississippi for an operation named JACKTWO. He followed up with a visit to Jackson State, where he toured the campus and examined the bullet-riddled walls. At one point he was overheard to comment: "And only twelve were struck?"

President Richard Nixon's Commission on Campus Unrest conducted a public inquiry into the Jackson State and Kent State killings, including thirteen days of hearings in Jackson. U.S. Senators Walter Mondale and Birch Bayh instigated a probe as well. The Commission issued a report that accused the Jackson police and the highway patrol of "unreasonable" overreaction, but there were no arrests because both the county grand jury and the federal grand jury concluded that legal action against the police would be "unjustified." As previously noted, Inspector Sullivan's assistance was of great value to me in conducting the investigation at the local level in Mississippi.

Later that year, I was transferred to FBI Headquarters in Washington, D.C. That was truly an experience. I was thirty-eight and starting another career. The metropolitan area was exactly what Marie and I thought it would be—expensive. I had spent my savings in Mississippi assisting my father who was dying of cancer in Henryetta. I was able during his remaining time to assist in paying his bills and making his life comfortable. The Bureau provided me with two weeks' vacation to spend time with my father and that meant a great deal to me.

Marie and I settled in Vienna, Virginia, after talking to several FBI officials. It was a place of beauty. Meeting new friends at the FBI Headquarters was a most enjoyable experience. I do not think I ever met anyone I did not like. Roy Moore once asked me if I had ever met anyone I did not like, and I said no, and that just about sums up my life.

The agents I began working with were all males—there were still no female supervisors at the FBI—but they were all very bright and friendly, and I soon found out that they were in the same predicament that I was in. Most did not want to come to

120

Washington. I ended up in a carpool with a great bunch of guys and we stuck together all during our Bureau career.

* * *

Shortly after moving to Washington, I went by Mississippi Senator James Eastland's office to say hello. Immediately, his staff wanted to know what I wanted. I told them that I merely wanted to pay my respects because I had met the senator two or three times in Mississippi.

Finally, after leaving the room for a few minutes, a skeptical staffer returned and said, "OK, the senator will see you."

I already knew he was in. I didn't make the trip until I knew that he was in his office. I work for the FBI.

Once I walked into his office, he just looked at me, saying nothing, waiting for me to ask for something. All our politicians at that level only expect people to come to them when they want something. I immediately told the senator, "I do not need anything—as you know I was in Mississippi for six years."

"I know those cases you worked," he answered. "I must say that when I did call the FBI, I got results and I knew that it was from you and Moore. Is there anything I can do for you?"

"Senator, I do not need anything. I just wanted you to know that I am now living in Washington."

"Good," he said. "If I need anything for Mississippi, I will give you a call." But he had a smirk on his face, as if to say that if he wanted something he'd just do it himself. Then he added, "Why don't you come over sometime and we'll have a little drink."

"Thank you very much senator, but I'm not sure that Director Hoover would approve of that."

"Well, he doesn't have to know everything you do."

"I said, "No, I think he does. We have that fear that we believe that the director knows everything we do."

"Well, he probably does," conceded the senator.

This visit began my relationship with the senator. When I came back to Washington from New York in later years, I called on him and I was always greeted kindly.

* * *

On March 8, 1971, a group calling itself Citizens Commission to Investigate the FBI broke into an FBI office in Media, Pennsylvania. The break-in occurred at a tiny, two-man office

121

during the celebrated Muhammad Ali-Joe Frazier fight, during which most of country was at home glued to their televisions. Entry was gained by the use of a single crowbar. More than 1,000 documents were stolen.

The burglars knew what they were looking for. They took files and other documents which were very embarrassing to the FBI. Some of the documents pertained to the counterintelligence program—codenamed COINTELPRO—that had been in place since 1956. Approved by Director Hoover, the program targeted the Communist Party, the Nazi Party, white hate groups, the Ku Klux Klan, and various black militant groups.

Within weeks, the documents began showing up in manila envelopes with no return address in the newsrooms of newspapers such as the *Washington Post* and the *New York Times*. The organization responsible for the break-in, Citizens' Commission to Investigate the FBI, alleged, among other things, that the FBI had fabricated derogatory information about targeted individuals and this information was sent to different parties with the intent of injuring their reputations.

Mr. Hoover was so embarrassed and livid over the break-in that he called for all stops to be pulled to find those responsible for the break-in. Mr. Hoover placed Roy Moore of Jackson in charge of the investigation. I had only been in Washington a short time. Roy called me and said that he needed me in Media. He knew that I would follow his orders and handle the grunt work. It was with regret that I told him I just could not do that.

I knew this upset him. He said, "Please think about it. I could have an agent pick you up and have you in Media in one day." I knew that he could have me transferred whether I wanted to or not, but I said, "Please, I'm settled. Marie and I have just purchased a home and paid double what we thought we would have to pay—a brand new home."

I went on to say that I was settled in a carpool with six terrific guys. I knew that if I went to Media it would be seven days a week again, with no sleep and I would leave my wife stranded to fend for herself in a new environment.

I asked him to please not make that telephone call to have me transferred and he honored my wishes, for which I have always respected him. After he got there he called me almost daily to give me a heads up, which I really didn't want to know since I had my own work that I was involved in. Even so, Roy liked to share, so I listened and tried to be supportive, even though my heart was not in it.

Later on in life, when I returned to Mississippi, he and I were the closest of friends. I had so many good years with him. As it turned out it would have been improper for me to participate in the Media investigation. None of us had any idea at the time where the matter would lead, but as I soon became one of the fall guys for the FBI's counterintelligence policies—and, as a result, I would come under investigation by the FBI for my activities in Mississippi.

The Media break-in was an eye-opener for many FBI agents across the country. It revealed that the documents approved by Mr. Hoover, if proven in federal court against FBI agents doing their duty, could result in agents losing everything they had ever worked for—their homes, bank accounts, whatever they had accumulated in the way of assets. It sent a cold reminder to FBI agents: Step back, because if you do your duty in domestic intelligence, you might be subjected to civil lawsuits.

* * *

J. Edgar Hoover died in May 1972, leaving behind unresolved questions about FBI wiretaps on Martin Luther King. The spying against the civil rights leader had begun in 1963, authorized by U.S. Attorney General Bobby Kennedy after Hoover told him that he needed the tapes to prove that King was involved with the Communist Party. No evidence of that was ever found, but the tapes, many of which were obtained by using microphones hidden under King's hotel beds, included graphic recordings of King's sexual activities. Some of the tapes were sent by the FBI to King, along with letters suggesting that suicide was the only way out for him to prevent public release of the tapes.

The agent in charge of the secret surveillance was William Sullivan, head of the Domestic Intelligence Division. He made copies of the tapes for the President, some members of Congress, and supervisory personnel at the FBI.

At FBI headquarters there was constant turmoil because Mr. Hoover and Sullivan were at odds over the leaking of the tapes on Dr. Martin Luther King to the news media. Eventually, the doors of Mr. Sullivan's office were locked while Mr. Sullivan was on vacation. When he returned he knew his days were numbered.

As the presidential campaign was heating up in the summer of 1972, just months after Mr. Hoover's death and a little more than a year after the Media break-in, five men wearing gloves and carrying walkie-talkies broke into the basement entrance of the Watergate office complex in Washington, D.C. After making their way to the office of the Democratic National Committee, they looked through files, dumping those they were not interested in onto the floor. They stuffed others into boxes which they planned to take with them. The attempted theft was thwarted by an alert night watchman who called the police.

When the intruders were booked at the police station, it was discovered that four of the burglars had previously worked as operatives for the Central Intelligence Agency and the fourth, James McCord, was employed at that time as the security coordinator for the Republican National Committee and President Nixon's re-election campaign.

The White House denied any knowledge of the break-in. Former U.S. Attorney General John Mitchell, who had resigned to oversee the Committee for the Re-Election of the President, said there was no place in the political process for such activities. Despite assurances by the White House and Republican Party leaders that neither was involved in the crime or had any knowledge of it, the Justice Department announced that the FBI had entered the case.

What a crushing blow Watergate was for all of us at Washington headquarters. Equally discouraging was to read in the *Washington Post* about what was going on inside the FBI. News articles dated October 10 and 11, 1972, reported that the FBI's investigation established that the Watergate bugging stemmed from a campaign of political spying directed by officials of the White House and the Committee to Re-elect the President. The burglary of the National Democratic Committee's headquarters not only had Washington reeling, but international capitals of the world were waiting to see the outcome and whether President Nixon could survive.

The article that I mentioned earlier that was published on October 10 was titled "FBI Find Nixon Aides Sabotaged

Democrats." A lengthy article by Carl Bernstein and Bob Woodward set out the FBI's findings that those of us within the FBI in Washington knew we had someone working inside the FBI at a very high level furnishing information to reporters. This was very upsetting to almost all of the agents with whom I associated. Each person that I knew was loyal to the FBI and loyal to Mr. Hoover. We could not understand anyone sabotaging the FBI by leaking information.

My old friend from Indianapolis, G. Gordon Liddy, was very much involved in this. As I knew back in the 1950s, Gordon was an extremely intelligent individual who knew his way around politically. He certainly knew the law, but he did not serve the president or John Mitchell well at the time.

It was sad that you had to be extremely careful of any remarks that you made in public or private because everyone was being scrutinized as a potential leaker. Our own small group discussed those matters each night as we traveled back to our homes in our carpool. We talked about who we suspected, what their motive was, and we had some interesting discussions. We all took an oath that we would be very careful not to discuss our suspicions with people beyond our carpool because we did not know who to trust.

As you might expect, the purloined FBI files taken from Media, Pennsylvania, and the Watergate break-in, attracted the attention of Congress. In the Senate, Senator Frank Church and in the House, Representative Otis Pike conducted intensive investigations and hearings on the activities of the White House, the FBI and other intelligence gathering agencies. All this was the result of the Watergate activities. The *Washington Post* and the *New York Times* published articles about surreptitious entries, black bag jobs, which had been carried out for years by the FBI without search warrants against the Communist Party, Socialists Workers Party and then later the Weather Underground.

The Church committee concluded that the FBI had fabricated derogatory information about targeted individuals and sent it to different parties. The U.S. Justice Department concluded that amends must be made for illegal FBI acts. It was also reported that some of the agents who took part in the COINTELPRO activities could possibly be exposed to costly civil lawsuits.

After a few months in Washington, I was transferred to the inspection staff and this was an enjoyable time. I worked with inspector Joe Ziel and we did interviews on wiretaps that had been authorized by various attorneys general. FBI officials wanted to know if they had been legal. Our most important interview was with Nicholas Katzenbach. Mr. Katzenbach was extremely kind and he provided the information on the wiretaps for when he was the attorney general. These were difficult decisions during that time and many attorneys general were under pressure regarding wiretaps. During my time in the inspection division, I had the opportunity to travel to Mexico and almost all of Central and South America. Those were exciting times.

*   *   *

In 1974, shortly after Gerald Ford was sworn in as president, the Government Accounting Office (GAO) concluded an audit of the FBI that resulted in a Justice Department investigation of numerous FBI agents thought to have been involved in warrantless break-ins of members of the Weathermen group. Faced with that reality, the FBI conducted its own investigation.

The GAO investigation came on the heels of the televised Watergate hearings that had resulted in the resignation of President Nixon. A federal grand jury was convened and FBI agents were subpoenaed to testify. Some agents admitted taking part in the break-ins, but said they were only following orders. The investigation led to several people, including myself. At that time I was the deputy assistant director of the criminal division.

The FBI conducted its own inquiry. Dick Long, section chief, was placed in charge of the FBI investigation. I was one of the agents under investigation. Dick Long and I had been friends for many years. We dined at each other's home and we had a close relationship. Long had an untenable task before him because he was investigating some agents like myself, who were considered friends.

*   *   *

One day agents came to my office, took all the files, including personal papers, at the request of the Justice Department. It was a sad time because you did not know who to trust. Of course, I continued my daily supervision that I was responsible for on cases occurring across the country. Although I was under deep pressure,

126

I never shirked from my duties and I must say it was a time when you knew who your friends were.

Roy Moore always said, Ingram, you can squeeze sweet juice out of a lemon, as a tribute to my people skills. That's why I was a witness hunter throughout my career because I could get at the truth. He reminded me of that because when you are under investigation by your peers everything seems to go awry. However, I knew I had not committed any violations.

Throughout, I had the complete support of assistant director Don Moore. Each day he said, "Jimbo, I will be glad when this nightmare is over for you. I have talked to Director Kelly and told him that I know you are innocent."

In handling my day-to-day activities, I was appointed to the first career board, along with Buck Levell. The career board interviews candidates who are in line to be promoted to other positions throughout the FBI, including assistant special agent in charge and special agent in charge of personnel to go to various field offices throughout the country. Also, we had a crisis management headquarters to review all the major cases that were going on across the country and we had many.

During this time, my good friend Wally LaPrade from New York was transferred to FBI headquarters in Washington. He and Director Kelly had a disagreement regarding some remarks Wally made about U. S. Attorney General Griffin Bell. Wally, who was truly a loyal Bureau employee, ended up being released from the FBI. This was a sad state of affairs as the Justice Department had gone after him over surreptitious entries.

Although I was under the gun each day because of the investigations, I would report early, do my job—and refuse to talk to the Justice Department's Civil Rights Division, which was conducting the agent investigations. I called upon an old friend, Jerris Leonard, who was the former assistant attorney general of the Civil Rights Division. He gave me the counsel that I needed and referred me to a former U.S. Attorney in Virginia.

I met with the attorney, paid him the advice fee, and he was then my attorney of record. But even though this new attorney was my attorney of record, Jerris was there for me at any hour for consultation. Based on their advice, I refused to be interviewed by the Justice Department, refused to be interviewed by the FBI, and refused to go before a grand jury.

Others had gone before the grand jury and I knew exactly what they were looking for. They were looking for statements they could use to file perjury charges against the agents. It was one agent's word against the others. I was asked to take a polygraph. On advice of attorney, I refused. That was unheard of in those days. I knew it was difficult for the officials above me to look at a person who refused to take a polygraph, but I had followed the polygraph my whole career and knew in many ways it was unreliable. It all depends on the operators. It is all about how the words or questions are arranged. My name was leaked to the *New York Times* and the *Washington Post* and I was castigated in articles for my refusal to cooperate with the grand jury. In that sense, there was a lynch mentality among some newspapers.

Jerris Leonard knew that I was innocent and he continued to give me sound advice. I knew that it was difficult for Assistant Director Jim Adams to continue to support me on the stance I had taken, but he never once questioned me about it.

Throughout the investigation of my involvement with COINTELPRO, I was elevated to be coordinator of Urban Guerrilla Warfare Activities, a promotion that was primarily the result of my success with the Ku Klux Klan in Mississippi. I was asked to supervise Black Nationalist and white hate group investigations in Anchorage, Denver, Honolulu, Kansas City, Las Vegas, Phoenix, and Salt Lake City.

*   *   *

In the fall of 1974, I was transferred to New York City to head up the FBI office there. After the melee in Washington, Marie and I were ready to go, ready for that transfer, ready to move on even if it was to New York. At that time, our son Jim was leaving for college and our sons, Stan and Steve, had graduated from Ole Miss, married, and entered law school.

I certainly never envisioned returning to New York City. However, arriving in New York, I realized instantly the beauty of the city by day and night. There was so much to do. So much to see. So much to accomplish if you were an FBI agent. Coming back to New York as the Special Agent in Charge was what many agents never expected to see when I left New York.

As I made my rounds to greet everyone, I'm sure they said, "I hope this guy is smarter than he was ten years ago when he was here." We'd laugh about those years and they'd laugh and shake their heads and say, "Ingram, we never thought we'd see you again in New York." And I'd say, "I never expected to be here, either."

It was a revelation to see so many old friends and so many individuals who had worked for me when I supervised their work in Mississippi. I was so happy to renew so many old acquaintances. New York is the largest FBI office in the country and offered so much because there were so many things from a criminal and intelligence gathering standpoint with both the Soviet Embassy and Cuban mission only two blocks from the office.

The first person who called on me was Inspector Joe Sullivan. He had retired and had a lot of time on his hands, but mentally he was extremely sharp. We talked about the old days in Mississippi, but mainly we discussed what was facing the United States in the early 1970s. He wanted to talk about the National Guard's actions at Kent State University, where he was sent to investigate the killings of four students after guardsmen opened fire on them.

We also talked about the Jackson State University demonstrations, where state police fired weapons and two people were killed. He was also really concerned about the Weathermen and the Students for a Democratic Society (SDS) and the violence associated with them in Chicago, Washington, Los Angeles, and New York.

We talked about the Media break-in where the COINTELPRO files were obtained. Then there were the problems in Washington, D.C., the pentagon being bombed, Watergate, and the rage that resulted in violent demonstrations across the country and the past riots in cities. Civil disorders were occurring so often that law enforcement was having a difficult time mounting a defense against those things.

Joe was also saddened by the death of Mr. Hoover, as he too loved Mr. Hoover. Joe was bothered by the disclosure that the Bureau had a "deep throat" and this person had not been identified, but was furnishing leaked information to Bernstein and Woodward, damaging the Bureau and damaging the U.S. government, including President Richard Nixon. He did not know how the FBI was going to manage all the problems that existed in the FBI because we still had tremendous will to get the job done.

The atmosphere was a sad one in some respects, but he prepared me for what would lie ahead in New York and later on in Washington, D.C.

I sought advice from many sections of the New York office and was called upon by several agents who had worked for me in Jackson, letting me know this was not Mississippi and agents did not work seven days a week as they had been "forced" to do in Mississippi; but after venting about the long hours they had to work in Mississippi each ended up saying they had enjoyed their stay there. One agent in particular, Joe Dertinger, a New York agent in every respect, went to Mississippi and with that New York accent became a hit with the chief of detectives, M. B. Pierce of the Jackson police department. M. B. would call me and say, "Send me all the Joe Dertinger's you have. I like that guy. He keeps me on my toes." I enjoyed his comments while I was in New York and we remained friends for many years.

I had a lot to learn in New York because New York police department officers were being killed, bombed, and maimed on a regular basis. I sought out Bob McCartin, a savvy no-nonsense agent who knew the streets. He knew the NYPD and introduced me around, which I very much appreciated. At that time, McCartin was working on the murders of two NYPD officers, Waverly Jones and Joe Piagentini. Their murders proved to be a planned execution by black extremists. He also updated me on the case involving NYPD officer Angel Poggi. He and other officers had been set-up to go to a particular building. As Poggi opened the door, a dynamite explosion occurred with fragments hitting Poggi in the face. He lost his right eye and limited use of his other eye, as well as being disfigured. In many ways they ruined his life. McCartin also briefed me on other cases, and I drew upon his experience during my time in New York.

On January 24, 1975, during the busy lunch hour, a bomb went off at Fraunces Tavern. Located at the tip end of Manhattan in the busy Wall Street area, the red-and-yellow brick restaurant was steeped in history. General George Washington had bid farewell to his troops at a dinner at Fraunces Tavern in 1783. For New Yorkers, it was an important link to the past. Four diners at the Anglers and Tarpon Club, located in a building adjacent to the tavern, were killed in the explosion.

I was in the FBI office at 201 East 690th Street when I received a telephone call about the bombing. I immediately left for the scene. Emergency vehicles and an ambulance were already there when I arrived. Men and women, covered in blood and dust, wandered about in the debris, dazed by the explosion.

I spotted a large contingent of NYPD officers and several FBI agents, who gave me a briefing on what had happened. I called Assistant Director Jim Adams at FBI headquarters and gave him what information I had. I told him that we would be working with the police department in connection with the bombing as well as all others that had occurred before this one. Mr. Adams told me to take charge and keep him apprised of the results.

I gathered the agents that were there and we began conducting interviews well into the night. At the scene, police discovered a note from the Fuerzas Armadas de Liberacion Nacional (FALN), a Puerto Rican national liberation group, in a telephone booth that read, "We . . . take full responsibility for the especially detotnated (sic) bomb that exploded today at Fraunces Tavern, with reactionary corporate executives inside."

Associated Press also received a call from a caller who boasted that the bomb was the handiwork of the FALN. This was a major special investigation because the FALN had really declared war as bombs were to follow in mid-Manhattan at the Chemical Bank branch, the Marine Midland branch, the Banco de Ponce branch, the Union Carbide building and the Lever Brothers building, all the result of dynamite. This was just the beginning of the FALN battle against the United States government.

The NYPD bomb squad members were all experienced because they handled bombings routinely throughout the city, but I knew having handled so many bombings in Mississippi that the evidence usually went up with the explosion. Sure, you could find that it was dynamite of a particular type, but most of your true evidence would be gone. We knew it was going to take a long time to end up with a solution in this case, but we had the personnel that could effectively handle this.

After drawing up a plan, we had to have some agents who wanted to work nights, days, week-ends, agents that could work with the police department and be able to handle the rigors of what we called a "special." I selected Mike Donovan as the supervisor of this group. Mike was a native New Yorker and the agents liked him. He knew several of the NYPD officers, and he could get the job done. It was decided that the case agent would be a young agent by the name of Don Wolfford. As I recall, he was from North Carolina and he was pound for pound a fighter. He was humorous in many ways and he worked well with other agents. He was free to select the agents he wanted and, as I recall, we ended up with 25-30 agents, some of whom had been at the scene that day, individuals who spoke Spanish and individuals who simply wanted to work the case. Wofford, I believe, coined the phrase FRANBOM as the code name. He and another young agent, Lou Vizi, had already teamed up together. So they were chosen to be the point for Donovan and myself.

Vizi, who was from Phillie I believe, has a daughter who is an agent, currently in the Phillie division. Since I had spent most of my career hunting witnesses, I knew this was what we would have to do. People do not come to you. People are inclined to keep to themselves if they see something they don't want get involved in. You have to go to them. Many times you pry it from them. We live in an era of people who do not want to get involved.

We certainly did not know what we had because the Weathermen, an anti-government group, mainly composed of white males and females, had been conducting bombings on the West Coast and the East Coast. Not long after the tavern bombing, FALN set off bombs in well-known businesses in New York City and Chicago, and other bombings in Washington D.C.

The bombings usually occurred in the middle of the night, usually between 3 and 4 a.m. The Weathermen concentrated their bombings on government installations to show their anti-war, anti-government agenda. We had surveillance at night, along with assistance from the NYPD, since bombs are mainly placed at night. We had a lot going for us, but still we were fighting an uphill battle.

Sometimes I left home and went to Manhattan in the middle of the night, driving an unmarked car. I would bring my wife, Marie, with me. We would park off of Fifth Avenue, where most of the large business establishments were located. We would set up surveillance, hoping that by chance I might see an individual carrying a bomb in a bag and placing the bag next to a building.

This was risky, having my wife along, but since we did not have female agents, I wanted it to look like we were just a male and a female waiting for someone. I brought two shotguns and a couple of revolvers in case I needed them, but I never encountered anyone during those surveillances. I did not tell the other agents because, rightfully so, they would say Ingram had lost his mind bringing his wife into a situation where both could be killed.

About that time I received a telephone call at my residence from a Spanish speaking male who threatened me, but we could not trace the call. We were certainly doing everything possible as an investigative unit, along with one of the finest police departments in the world, but we were not gathering those witnesses we needed to bring us the identities of the bombers.

Pressure was brought to bear on myself and others. Assistant Director Adams, whom I respected, was questioned about why these bombs were occurring across the country and we had not identified suspects or made arrests. In December, around Christmas, 1975, a bomb exploded at LaGuardia Airport, late in the evening, killing eleven people and injuring seventy-five others. Our bomb squad still did not have an answer.

The FBI office in New York had a tremendous team, composed of Wally LaPrade, Bill Beane, Phil McNiff and Tom Emery. This was the Big Apple. The Big Time. We dealt with organized crime, murders for hire, kidnappings, multiple bank robberies, big fraud cases, every type of crime imaginable.

Around this time we had a major case, the kidnapping of Sam Bronfman, the 21-year-old son of multi-millionaire Edgar Bronfman, the Seagram's whiskey heir. Because Edgar Bronfman was North American chairman of the World Jewish Congress and a vocal supporter of Israel, it was first thought that the kidnapping might have been politically motivated.

After we put considerable resources into solving the case, Sam was returned safely. The two men responsible for his kidnapping were captured, but they were acquitted of kidnapping by a jury and convicted of lesser charges of grand larceny through extortion. Asked by news reporters after the trial why they did not believe Sam's testimony that he was kidnapped, jurors admitted they bought into the defense's allegation that Sam was one of the defendants' homosexual lovers and had staged the kidnapping as a hoax. The Bronfman family called the acquittal a miscarriage of justice. The FBI investigated the possibility of a hoax and found no evidence of one.

Times being what they were at the FBI, I was most appreciative to receive a laudatory letter from Director Kelley about the Bronfman investigation: "You handled your various obligations commendably incident to the investigation of the kidnapping case ... the laudable results achieved with the safe return of the victim, the identification and apprehension of the subjects, and recovery of the ransom can be attributed in a large measure to the splendid leadership you afforded this sensitive operation. The fine job that you did for the FBI is something in which you may take a great deal of pride."

The distraction from the FALN investigation was just one of many we experienced. Crime simply wasn't interested in taking a holiday. The FALN was a small part of our workload, but a major one. We convinced Special Agent Paul Brana to take over the reins of the FALN investigation. Paul was probably one of the tougher guys you'd ever meet, a person you'd want with you if you were in an alley and had trouble. The agents respected him because he had worked some big-time cases in the New York office. I enjoyed working with Paul, and we knew eventually that if we kept the pressure, we would solve the FALN case, which we eventually did.

*   *   *

In August 1975 an Asian male and an American male attempted to enter the United States from Canada. U.S. Customs detained the Asian male because he could not furnish proper identification. The American male furnished identification showing an address in New York City and was released. After several interviews, the Asian male admitted being a member of the Japanese Red Army (JRA) and admitted he was entering the United States to establish liaison and study with the Black Panther Party. He said he had arrived in Canada during the summer of 1974 with a female Black Panther Party member who preceded him to New York City, where she had obtained a false identification for the American male.

The JRA was an international terrorist group formed in the early 1970s to overthrow the Japanese government. In time it expanded its goals to instigate world revolution. Prior to 1975, it had carried out a massacre in 1972 at Lod Airport in Israel, attempted to take

134

over the U.S. Embassy in Kuala Lumpur, and conducted two Japanese airliner hijackings. They were a dangerous group to have running loose in America.

I had been the Special Agent in Charge of the New York office for about one year when this occurred. Because of the timing of the events associated with the detainees we concluded that the JRA could be mounting a terrorist operation against Japanese Emperor Hirohito, who was scheduled to make his first visit ever to America in September 1975.

Informants told us that two Japanese-American females, one from New York, the other from Los Angeles, were in New York City to undertake or facilitate actions against the Emperor. A background investigation disclosed that an associate of the Asian-American woman based in California had purchased an automatic rifle and two revolvers and had moved to an undisclosed location in New York. We immediately furnished this information to the Secret Service and the State Department, although there were no warrants or evidence to pinpoint threats against the Emperor.

The Secret Service concluded that there was evidence enough to obtain a search warrant to search the Brooklyn apartment of the women. They found numerous rifles, including two semi-automatic AR-180s and one revolver, as well as cross bows. The Secret Service raid garnered front-page headlines, and television and radio also covered the arrests. Secret Service officials said that the arrests, which were done to protect the life of the Emperor, were based on information furnished by the FBI.

I was asked to be the liaison with the Secret Service and the New York City Police for the visit of the Emperor and Empress to insure their safety. I assisted in around-the-clock surveillances of individuals affiliated with terrorist organizations and made use of about thirty FBI agents to accomplish this.

After the Emperor's visit concluded without incident, I received a letter from FBI Director Clarence Kelley commending me for my contribution to a successful conclusion: "As a result of the exceptional leadership you afforded this sensitive operation, as well as your professionalism and meticulous attention to detail, you contributed immensely to the results attained. I am certainly appreciative of your valuable services which have been of substantial benefit to our organization."

Inside the envelope with the letter was a check for $150, an incentive award for my work. It was the thought that counts. Some folks may feel I was grossly under-compensated for saving the Emperor's life. Others may feel that I was over-compensated for saving the life of the man who, as emperor, approved plans for the infamous sneak attack on Pearl Harbor. Whatever my personal feelings about the emperor, it was my job to protect him while he was in this country. His assassination on American soil would have done irreparable harm to this country's image abroad.

* * *

In 1968, Eldridge Cleaver, Black Panther Party Minister of Information, led an ambush of Oakland police officers during which two officers were wounded. Cleaver, who had served time for assault with intent to murder in California's San Quentin and Folsom prisons, was an admitted serial rapist of white women, acts he once described in an essay as "an insurrectionary act. It delighted me that I was defying and trampling upon the white man's law . . . defiling his women." Charged with attempted murder in the attack on Oakland police, he jumped bail and fled to Cuba, where he lived in exile for a time, supported by the Cuban and North Vietnam Communist governments before moving on to Algeria and then finally to Paris, France.

In 1975, while I was assigned to the New York Office, the FBI got word that Cleaver wanted to surrender and return to the United States to face the charges against him. The question was why? Was it a ploy to obtain a passport, after which he would disappear into the night? Was there a secret agenda? In his second memoir, *Soul on Fire,* Cleaver subsequently attempted to explain his change in heart:

> **I began to experience a severe depression. Perhaps I have been crazy all my life, but I never went around depressed or brooding or tormented or anything like that. In this situation in France, I began to be terribly depressed. I began to feel completely, totally useless, burdened. I began to put a lot of pressure on my wife with the idea of driving her away and forcing her to go back to the United States and take the children. I was the obstacle.**

> **Kathleen had never been arrested in her life. My children had never been arrested. They were free. I was the fugitive and it was my fault we were locked out; and I began to feel guilty to the extent that I could hardly face them. To be around them I felt miserable, guilty, seeing the emptiness that had become our life.**

Cleaver began his journey home by strolling into a Paris law office to ask attorney Carl Salans, a survivor of Auschwitz, to contact the American government and arrange for his surrender. Salans questioned him about his reasons, privately wondering about his sanity; but once he was convinced that he was of sound mind he set the process in motion by contacting the U.S. Justice Department, at that time under the direction of Attorney General Edward Levi.

I was asked to travel to Paris and accept Cleaver's surrender, and then escort him back to New York, where he would enter the justice system. I chose a black FBI agent to accompany me. For some in the black community, Cleaver was a revered hero, albeit a tarnished one. For law enforcement officers, he was a scourge, someone who had waged war against them. During my years in Mississippi, I had grown accustomed to walking a fine line between opposing views.

Once we arrived in Paris, our first stop was the U.S. Embassy. Because of the State Department's concerns about his motives for asking for a passport, it was decided that the embassy would provide a letter of transit instead of a passport. It was a one-way ticket to America. Cleaver found that solution perfectly acceptable.

I met with Cleaver before our departure and let him know what to expect.

"Will I be handcuffed with shackles on my legs?" he asked.

His question was more of a plea than an inquiry. I thought a moment and then answered, "You are a fugitive, but you have voluntarily submitted to return to the United States to face a California court. I will not handcuff you as long as we are on the plane."

"Thank you," he said, and then expressed his fear that he would be shackled.

"No, you will not."

We did not know until we boarded the plane it would be almost completely filled with reporters who had attended a European conference at which President Gerald Ford was in attendance. The reporters were pleased that Cleaver was on board, confident that they would have full access to him throughout the long flight to New York.

When approached by the reporters, Cleaver told them that he was in my custody. I had already counseled him about being careful about what he said to reporters, explaining that he was returning to face a California court in which anything he said on the plane could be used against him. He asked if I would handle the situation and explain that he would not be making a statement during the flight. When I was approached by the reporters I passed along his message.

We had a nice conversation on our way to New York. He certainly was a changed man from the time of his violent days as a leader of the Black Panther Party. After leaving the United States, he realized what a great country it is and that he should cherish the fact that he had had many opportunities as a citizen. This was further brought home to him after he went to Algeria, where the government took care of him. He could see how other people had to live. He wanted to come back, do what he had to do to clear himself, and start a new life, which he did.

On the flight I explained that he would have to be handcuffed upon our departure from the plane, but that we could cover the handcuffs with a coat to shield his handcuffs from the photographers and we would take a back entrance from the terminal where a car would be waiting for him. At least that was the plan. I was advised that there were a large number of reporters waiting for us, hoping to get interviews with Cleaver, or at the very least photographs of him handcuffed.

Cleaver wrote about what happened next:

> **When the plane landed in New York, a warrant for my arrest was read to me as soon as my feet hit the ground. I was placed under arrest, my hands forced behind my back and handcuffed there. My heart started racing as the FBI agents grabbed me by each arm and led me through a**

door into a room filled with journalists. Flashbulbs and cameras blinking and flashing, they tossed hundreds of questions at me simultaneously, while stampeding and trampling upon each other. The agents plowed a path through the center of the journalists, using me as the plow. I thought I was going to get trampled—what I hated about handcuffs was how vulnerable they make you to any outside force; I kept thinking of how Lee Harvey Oswald got assassinated while wearing them— but we finally reached the FBI station at the airport where I was fingerprinted and photographed.

Not until we reached the office of a U.S. commissioner, where he was arraigned on the fugitive warrant, did we remove the handcuffs. There were exchanges between a U.S. Attorney, Cleaver's lawyer, and the commissioner about his bail, whether it should remain at the 1968 level of $50,000 or be raised to $100,000, which the U.S. Attorney's office recommended. The commissioner suggested that if Cleaver did not resist extradition to California, he would leave it at $50,000 and allow California authorities to decide whether a higher bail was appropriate.

Cleaver said he had returned voluntarily and had no intention of resisting extradition to California. Then there was the matter of whether he should be handcuffed for the journey to California. Federal marshals said that handcuffs were mandatory and they could not waive that requirement. The Justice Department solved that problem by arranging for guards from the Federal Bureau of Prisons to transport him without handcuffs.

Once he reached California his bail was increased to $100,000. Because he did not have the money, he remained in custody for nine months, until such time as friends were able to obtain the funds to secure his release. Ultimately, his case was resolved and he was sentenced to probation for assault. Meanwhile, he renounced his radical past and became a born-again Christian and an active member of the Republican Party. For several years after my encounter with Cleaver, we exchanged Christmas cards.

*   *   *

My sojourn in New York turned out to be a sad time for me. In 1976, while I was heading up the New York office, the ACLU filed a lawsuit against me, Roy Moore, who had retired from the FBI in 1975, and an acting agent Tom Fitzpatrick of the Alexander, Virginia office. The charge was violating the civil rights of Mohammed Kenyatta, a black activist from Pennsylvania. Kenyatta had joined with the ACLU in filing a civil suit alleging we conspired through political motives and racial animosity to force Kenyatta to leave the State of Mississippi in mid-1969, thus depriving him of free speech and due process of law and violating his constitutional rights. The lawsuit was not filed against the FBI, the Justice Department, or any government agency, but against the three of us as individuals for large monetary awards. It was alleged we had targeted Kenyatta under a program code named COINTELPRO (counterintelligence program), the purpose of which was to prevent the coalition of black militant nationalist groups.

Muhammed Kenyatta came to Mississippi in 1966 to work with the Child Development Group of Mississippi, a job he held until 1967. The following year, he enrolled as a student at Tougaloo College, a black institution of higher learning located just outside Jackson. About a year after enrolling he was suspended for non-payment of his tuition fees. Despite his suspension, Kenyatta remained on campus and engaged in political activity. He was a member of the Tougaloo Political Action Committee and the Jackson Human Rights Project.

Sometime around Christmas 1967, the Jackson field office of the FBI placed Kenyatta's name and biographical information on the FBI's "Rabble Rouser Index," later renamed the "Agitator Index." The index provided FBI field offices around the country with a reference summary of information on individuals who had established a pattern of traveling around the country to participate in demonstrations or rallies where violence had occurred.

We felt Kenyatta fell in that category. As a result, we maintained surveillance of him and gathered information about him from informants and published sources. According to FBI directives the purpose of COINTELPRO was to "expose, disrupt, misdirect, discredit, or otherwise neutralize the activities of black nationalist, hate-type organizations and groupings, their leadership,

140

spokesmen, membership, and supporters, and to counter their propensity for violence and civil disorder." Following those official guidelines, the Jackson FBI office participated in that program.

In April 1969, while Kenyatta was still involved in campus political life, we composed a fictitious letter made to appear as if it had originated from an actual Tougaloo organization, the Tougaloo College Defense Committee. The letter asked Kenyatta to stay away from the campus until his conduct improved. He was warned that if the advice in the letter went unheeded, authorities would be contacted and measures would be taken. Soon after receiving the letter, Kenyatta left Mississippi. In his lawsuit, he said he left because of the letter.

Around that time, we were contacted by an attorney representing the Episcopal Church, who inquired about the Jackson Human rights Project. The request originated with members of the church who wanted to make contributions to the group. In response, Agent Fitzpatrick referred the attorney to numerous sources of derogatory information about the group, including newspaper articles. A report grew out of the attorney's request and it was provided to the individuals making the inquiry as well as myself, Fitzpatrick and Special Agent in Charge Roy Moore. As a result of the report, the Episcopal Church General Assembly voted to discontinue support of the Jackson Human Rights Project. Kenyatta claimed in his lawsuit that the report was the sole reason for the church's failure to renew funding.

The lawsuit came as a blow to me because the Justice Department already had an investigation of me at the time, also concerning COINTELPRO. The lawsuit prompted a second investigation. Tom Fitzpatrick, who is now deceased, was without a doubt the best all-around agent I had ever worked with or supervised. He was a former army captain and Georgetown University graduate. Tom was everything that a person would want in an FBI agent. He was straight as an arrow, a man of Catholic faith. I knew we would suffer in the lawsuit, but would eventually win. The main thing was that we were sued in federal court and if we lost we could lose everything we had gathered over the years. The lawsuit was meant to harass FBI agents into ceasing any investigative activities.

Our attorneys filed a motion for summary judgment on the basis that we, as FBI agents, had qualified immunity. That was our best hope to make the lawsuit go away. Unfortunately, U.S. District Judge Dan Russell felt otherwise. He denied our motion for summary judgment

In his opinion, Judge Russell ruled that the FBI's investigation of Kenyatta could have led to the "disruption and harassment of not lawfully exercising his First Amendment rights." Further, he wrote: "The record before the Court supports the inference that in targeting the plaintiff in COINTELPRO, the defendants were reacting to the content of the plaintiff's speeches. Additionally the defendants apparently based their actions on the premise that the plaintiff's associates were extremists. Furthermore, the purpose of the forged letter was to "give him the impression that he has been discredited at the Tougaloo College campus and is no longer welcomed there . . . It may possibly also cause him to decide to leave Mississippi."

For my co-agents and myself it was a devastating ruling because it meant that simply carrying out orders was not enough to protect us individually from potentially disastrous lawsuits.

EDITOR'S NOTE

COINTELPRO was a decade old before it was used by FBI agents in Mississippi against the Ku Klux Klan. However, the efforts in Mississippi were directed against white extremists and were tame when compared to those used by agents in other jurisdictions against blacks.

For example, agents in the St. Louis office sent an anonymous letter to the wife of a black leader stating that he had been "making it" with other women. In another instance the husband of a white woman who worked with a biracial organization received a letter from agents stating she was "shucking and jiving" with black men. The couple separated as a result of the letter.

J. Edgar Hoover justified the program because he felt that the Communist Party and the Black Panther Party were the two biggest threats to the internal security of the country. It was not a big leap for agents to transfer the tactics that targeted the Black Panther Party to ordinary black activists who demonstrated for civil rights.

So ingrained was that way of thinking that Hoover used the same psychological manipulation against his ideological enemies in the White

House. Once Hoover realized that Richard Nixon's "palace guard"—John Ehrlichman, specifically—was restricting his access to the president, he used sketchy information he obtained from a reporter to direct an FBI investigation into the highest levels of the White House on the grounds that Nixon's inner circle were homosexuals and thus a threat to national security. This false revelation was made by Hoover to his right-hand man, Assistant Director William Sullivan, who later disclosed the information to author Curt Gentry in an interview for his bestselling book, *J. Edgar Hoover: The Man and The Secrets*. Ironically, Sullivan is considered by many to be the architect of COINTELPRO.

When Hoover told Nixon about the rumors, the president was stunned. Hoover told Nixon he would have Assistant Director Mark Felt conduct a discreet investigation. Felt reported back that he found no evidence of homosexual activity among top aides in the White House. The case was subsequently closed. However, as a COINTELPRO tactic used by the government against itself, it was highly effective. It destroyed Ehrlichman's image of invincibility and it brought Hoover into Nixon's confidence, which was the goal all along.

—James L. Dickerson

*   *   *

In 1978, I was transferred back to Washington.

The problems in Washington with the resignation of President Nixon, the Watergate fallout, the Deep Throat revelations were affecting all of us. The erosion of morale in the FBI was apparent. A decision by Attorney General Edward Levi to notify several hundred persons that they were targets of past FBI harassment campaigns to disrupt militant political groups on the political right and left certainly added to our problems. All this stemmed from testimony before Senate intelligence committees in 1975.

I truly did not want to leave New York at that time because we had several matters still unresolved, particularly the FALN. It is interesting to note, though, even though we had not solved our problem in New York, an active investigation of the FALN was underway in San Juan and Chicago. Just a few years later, we were able to crack the FALN and I was fortunate to be the special agent in charge in Chicago at the time.

But now I am in route to Washington D.C.

I reported to FBI headquarters and I continued an excellent working relationship with Assistant Director Jim Adams and others. I had the pleasure of working with some outstanding young FBI executives. One assistant director, Don Moore, whom we called Big Daddy, was one of Clarence Kelly's closest friends. Don and his wife, Charlotte, had Director Kelly to their home weekly and Director Kelly enjoyed playing cards with Don and Charlotte and their daughters. They had a tremendous working relationship and Director Kelly had a deep faith in Don because he knew that Don would tell him the truth.

Also, during that time, I had a very close relationship with Lee Coldwell, who later became one of my closest friends, as well as Buck Revell, an old friend who was born and raised a few miles from me in Oklahoma. I had experience in bombings and the reason for my transfer was strictly the fact that the U.S. government was getting geared to celebrate its 200th birthday. From the president on down, people were very concerned. We had to make Capitol Hill and all of Washington safe to celebrate the founding of this country. We were concerned with actions by those people who had been committing bombings. We certainly made every effort to make 1976 a safe year and through all our investigative efforts with other agencies, we had a safe and secure birthday celebration at the nation's capital.

The following year, as part of my duties as a terrorism specialist, I went to the U.S. Air Force Air Command and Staff College at Maxwell Air Force Base in Alabama to instruct students on the characteristics of terrorism. I was pleased when the Commandant, Major General William Nicholson, wrote Director Kelley a letter regarding my visit. In the letter, Nicholson wrote: "Please extend our sincere appreciation to Deputy Assistant Director James O. Ingram for his superb presentation . . . his informative and incisive articulation of the role of the Federal Bureau of Investigation in preserving our national security provided our students with an excellent insight into the contemporary threat posed by revolutionaries and terrorists."

* * *

For the next several years, I submitted to depositions to the ACLU, and these were not happy times. The ACLU always came across in a mean-spirited way, even though you cooperated and were truthful in your answers. In my opinion, they still had a sense of "hatred" of the FBI, at least the individuals that we dealt with.

Things were so bad during this time that even though I left my residence in Virginia at 5:30 each morning to get to work to handle my assignments and then return to my residence at night, I could not openly discuss with my wife the personal things associated with the ACLU lawsuit or the Justice Department investigation of me. We went on long walks outside our residence to discuss those things because I never knew if my telephone or my home could be wiretapped.

In February 1978, Federal Judge William H. Webster became director of the FBI. What a gracious gentleman. He was a no-nonsense, straight-forward, fact-seeking director. He did not want any spin on the subject. He wanted the facts. Not long after his arrival in Washington, we had a tremendous snowstorm. I got up at 3 a.m., saw the snow, put chains on my tires, and struggled to get to FBI headquarters. Only a handful of people were able to make it in that day. Judge Webster was one of those who made it in. Although there was a blizzard going on, we opened shop because we were dealing with field offices all across the country that needed answers on certain criminal investigations on that day.

Judge Webster called down and I answered the telephone.

"Ingram do you have a full staff?" he asked.

"Judge, I'm it.

"I'm it also, I think."

The judge saw my work ethic and probably thought maybe this guy is not as bad as I'm hearing or he would have stayed home today. Judge Webster and I have been friends for years. I had the honor of having dinner with him in 2007 in Orlando, Florida.

Jim Ingram

10

MASS SUICIDE IN GUYANA

In November 1978, I was still in Washington, D.C. as the deputy assistant director in the criminal division and was working November 18 when we received information of the suicide/murder in the South American country of Guyana of more than 900 members of Jim Jones's followers. Jim Jones was a madman, but he was also the spiritual leader of the Peoples Temple, a racially integrated church founded in Indianapolis, Indiana in 1956.

Prior to starting up the Peoples Temple, he built a Methodist-based Pentecostal ministry named Wings of Deliverance. To finance his church he imported small monkeys from South America and sold them door-to-door on a bicycle equipped with a cage. Many of the individuals to whom he sold monkeys, impressed by his animated but sincere sales pitch, began attending his church. In 1954, the *Indianapolis Star* ran a front-page story about Jones's refusal to claim a shipment of sick monkeys that had arrived at the airport addressed to him. Jones quickly learned that publicity and public outreach were the way to go to build a strong ministry. You also might say that he subscribed to P. T. Barnum's observation that "nobody ever lost a dollar by underestimating the taste of the American public."

In 1966 the Peoples Temple relocated to Redwood Valley, California, where it proceeded to develop into a communist-style communal church that stressed the social benefits of living and working together in harmony. Throughout the teachings of Jim Jones was a strong anti-government current that prompted him in 1973 to lease jungle land from the Guyanese government for the purpose of establishing his own city to be named the Jonestown Agricultural Settlement. He wanted to get as far away as possible from United States government regulation.

As workers in Guyana labored to clear the jungle, Jim Jones worked tirelessly to build his Peoples Temple into a religious movement that had a national impact. Through donations and other schemes, he became close friends with politicians, governors, mayors, and others in the public eye.

Since Redwood Valley was located less than thirty miles from San Francisco, he focused much of his public relations on that city. He sent fifty dollars to the family of a slain San Francisco police officer and received a letter of thanks from the police chief. He contributed to political campaigns and received letters of appreciation from politicians all across the country, including President Richard Nixon and numerous congressmen. Not immune to Jim Jones's manipulations was FBI Director J. Edgar Hoover, who sent him a letter of thanks for a gift of Christmas candy. Jones felt he could do anything that he wanted to do, and get away with it.

In 1976, though his friendships, he was appointed to the San Francisco human rights commission and through the influence of Mayor George Moscone was elected chairman of the San Francisco housing commission. He was also extremely friendly with Eldridge Cleaver of the Black Panther Party, and had contacts at the federal, state, and local level. Cult and cult-like groups have been part of our history for many years. Free sex, booze, drugs were rampant, but you did not expect to see this coming from a reverend such as Jim Jones.

Reverend Jones is a prime example of a madman gone completely insane. He was in complete control of the Peoples Temple and he was able to convince the poor, black and white, the elderly, and the young desperate for a religion that would justify their spiritual and physical cravings, to join him at his Peoples Temple. He took advantage, in many cases, by taking property signed over to the church, along with their money, and it was sad to see exactly what he could do with people.

At his command, he would have sex with anyone within his flock. Church members could not refuse. He had sex with the wives of members, and their husbands knew of this but could do nothing about it. Some undoubtedly saw their wives' infidelities as a gift to God.

Federal and state agencies certainly received complaints about the Peoples Temple. Before long Reverend Jones and the church came under investigation by the IRS and FBI for extortion and tax evasion. In 1977, a series of published exposes about the church, prompted Reverend Jones to seek sanctuary in Guyana. We could never figure out how he could convince over a thousand people to follow him to South America, particularly deep in the jungle. Guyana was formerly British Guyana. With the assistance of the Guyana government, he was able to take his people to a place where they were helpless to ever escape because he had guards surrounding the compound. The work at the compounds was strenuous and often painful. They were constantly being watched. And any violation was dealt with severely by the guards.

After receiving many complaints from families in his district, a courageous U.S. Congressman, Leo Ryan, led a fact-finding mission to the settlement in November 1978 to investigate alleged human rights violations. Ryan was accompanied by NBC reporters, Tim Reiterman, a journalist with the *San Francisco Examiner*, who had written extensively about Jonestown; and a *Time* magazine reporter.

Jim Jones had prepared his flock for the visit by stating this group was coming to kill them—or at the very least, take their children away from them. His followers were warned to be careful about what they said to the strangers. Quickly, a wave of hysteria swept among Jonestown residents.

On the first day of the group's arrival, at a meeting between Ryan and Jones supporters, a man came up behind Ryan and grabbed him around the neck, sticking a knife against his throat. Ryan froze in place, and the man voiced his profanity-riddled desire to see him dead. The man was subdued by bystanders and Ryan escaped with only minor injuries and a torn shirt spotted with blood. But the die had been cast. The residents of Jonestown were past the point of no return.

At around that time, Guyana police showed up at Jonestown after receiving reports of gunfire. They stopped at a one of the houses to ask questions. Seeing the police outside, a mother herded her three children into a bathroom, fearful that the police were there to take them away from her. In his book, *Raven: The Untold Story of the Rev. Jim Jones and His People*, journalist Tim Reiterman described what happened next:

Amos was shaking and uncontrollably nervous. She turned to Beikman [one of the males at the house], saying she was going to kill the children before the police took them. She pulled Christa (11 years of age) to her, and holding her by the face, she slit her throat. Christa fell screaming to the floor, her legs kicking up spasmodically. Chuck Beikman watched helplessly. He could not, would not, interfere. Sharon then reached for Martin (8 years of age), who began to slink away from her, but she caught up with him, held him by his nose and mouth, and slit his throat, too.

Beikman froze as she ordered him to kill Stephanie (9 years of age); he administered only a superficial cut and let her drop to the floor. Amos, meanwhile, turned to her daughter Liane (21 years of age) and handed her the knife.

'Here,' she cried, ''you've got to do me.'

And as Liane cut, Sharon urged, 'Harder, harder.' She took Liane's hands, and with her own hands guiding them, managed to complete her own suicide, murmuring, 'Thank you, Father,' as she collapsed to the floor.

Liane then turned the knife on herself. With some difficulty she slashed her own throat, before she fell convulsing to the floor.

The killings and suicides were just the beginning of an unimaginable nightmare. Realizing that the situation at Jonestown was escalating out of control and he would have to bring his visit to an abrupt end, Ryan announced that it was time to return to the States.

As the delegation was fleeing to board the airplane to return to California, a truckload of armed guards arrived and fired upon the departing Americans. Ryan was killed and four others met their death, and I recall at least two others were wounded.

Later that day, Jones, who always appeared to be in a drug-induced haze, called the 913 residents, including 276 children, to a meeting and after hours of talking they were served a cyanide-laced grape-flavored soft drink. It was a mass suicide. Subsequently, Jones was found dead with a gunshot wound to his head, although it was never determined if he committed suicide or was shot by someone else.

News of the mass suicide was broadcast all over the world, particularly since a U.S. Congressman was killed and others in the news media killed or wounded.

Guyana, as I recall, had a socialist government that allowed very few people into their country. In view of the fact that the murder of a U.S. congressman was a federal violation, the FBI was asked to go to Guyana. At that time, Don Moore was the assistant director and Dan Shaffer was the designated case agent. Upon confirming with the director and associate director, we planned to send personnel from the FBI identification division into the country.

We had been told that the bodies in the terrific heat in Guyana were bloated and some could not be moved. We knew we would have to use other measures to identify the individuals so that the families could be told if their loved ones had perished through the mass suicide and murder by Jim Jones.

We soon discovered that Guyana did not want FBI investigators in their country. The state department and other government officials attempted to persuade Guyana to allow us to come in and conduct a proper investigation to see exactly what had happened. We had our passports and we were ready to depart. U.S. officials wanted us to go there and I was prepared, along with the others, to proceed to the jungles of Guyana. After several conferences, Guyana firmly said no, although they did ask for our help identifying the bodies.

At the request of the Guyana government, our fingerprint experts proceeded to Guyana. The bodies had been black bagged and the only way possible to identify them would be to remove a certain finger from a body so that the finger could then be matched for a proper identification. The fingers were brought back to the United States and once preliminary matches were accomplished the bodies of U.S. citizens were then transported to Dover Air Force base in Delaware and placed in cold storage, where further identification could be undertaken and families notified.

This was a sad episode of our history, where you had an individual who had done church work his entire life, beginning as a teenager. Sadly, he went off center and took advantage of the poor, the elderly and even the young men and women who at first believed in him. Almost all his followers perished in the jungle. Those who did not go to Guyana, but had been acquainted with the Peoples Temple, furnished facts about the grimness of being around Jones—his drug use, his habits, his mistreatment of men and women. He was able to skillfully convince people at the highest levels of government that he was doing God's work. Sadly, he was not.

Congressman Ryan gave his life to travel to the jungle of South America on a fact-finding mission. Not enough people listened at the time in San Francisco to stop Jones. Unfortunately, we have seen other cult leaders in this country over the last few years rise to prominence. When people attempt to highlight human rights violations, or try to uncover the truth, those individuals often are verbally attacked and the matter never goes any further.

For years, there have been jokes made about drinking cyanide-laced Cool-Aid and those bad-taste jokes still are frequently heard. Only two people were ever brought to trial in this case. One was convicted in a U.S. court of the murder of Ryan (he was paroled in 2002). The second person plead guilty in Guyana for his role in the throat slashing of Sharon Amos's children. The U.S. government followed the money trail (some individuals, at Jim Jones's request, fled before the violence began with suitcases filled with money) and did recover some of the funds stashed away by Jim Jones and his followers.

To this day there are those in this country that subscribe to his anti-government philosophy. Some of his teachings have come true—he predicted the resurgence of the Ku Klux Klan and right-wing militia groups, and that has come to pass—but for the most part he is recognized as a mass murderer who ordered the deaths of innocent individuals whose worst crimes were wanting to believe in someone or something larger than themselves. That is nothing new in human history, but when it results in the deaths of innocent children it is particularly tragic.

Rev. Jim Jones FBI task force for investigation of Guyana suicides, with Jim Ingram second from right

11

CODE NAME WOODMUR

In May 1979, Chief Judge John Wood of the U.S. District Court in San Antonio, Texas, received a threatening letter. He didn't think too much about it. His job was to send the bad guys to prison—and he excelled at it. Nicknamed "Maximum John," he had a preference for maximum sentences for serious drug offences, especially if violence was an ingredient in the crime. At that time in Texas, organized crime elements felt they had an unspoken gentleman's agreement with some prosecutors and judges that, if convicted, they would not get the book thrown at them. They calculated minimum jail sentences as a cost of doing business. If they got caught, they got caught—no big deal.

Judge Wood did not subscribe to that line of thinking. His prison sentences reflected the unspoken belief "that if you can't do the time, don't do the crime." He was dismissive of the threatening letter, but nonetheless federal marshals were assigned to him and other federal officials thought to be at risk of harm. A big bear of a man at 6 foot 3, Wood told his law clerk, according to author Gary Cartwright, that he thought the marshals were a waste of money: "I was shot at during World War II and I didn't like it, but there was nothing I could do about it. If they're going to kill you, they're going to kill you. We've got a job to do, so let's do it."

Early on the morning of May 29, Judge Wood's wife, Kathryn, went outside to pull their station wagon out of the carport and noticed that she had a flat tire. Their plan had been for Wood to follow her to a repair shop in his car, where they would leave the station wagon for minor work, and he would then give her a lift downtown before going to his office. The flat tire changed all that. Notified of the flat tire, he left the townhouse at 8:30 a.m. and opened the driver's door of his car. A shot rang out from a .240 Wetherby Mark V rifle. The bullet struck him in the back, severing his spine and fragmenting into dozens of tiny pieces. He fell to the pavement, landing onto his back.

Hearing the shot, Kathryn ran outside and saw her husband on the ground. She lifted his head, cradling it in her arms. She asked who had shot him. Though his eyes were open he did not respond. She ran back inside and called 911. Once they arrived, paramedics determined that he was not breathing and did not have a heartbeat. They initiated CPR. Then they rushed him to the nearest hospital, where he was declared dead on arrival.

It was the first assassination of a federal judge in America in over one hundred years. State, local and federal investigators poured over his docket for clues. One of the cases that caught their attention was the one against Jimmy Chagra, a well-known gambler and drug kingpin, who was facing drug trafficking charges in Wood's court. Courthouse watchers knew that if Chagra was convicted he would likely receive the maximum sentence from "Maximum John"—life imprisonment.

Investigators concentrated on Chagra, the son of a Lebanese American rug merchant who lived in El Paso, Texas. With two brothers who had forged successful careers as lawyers, one of whom specialized in defending individuals charged with drug offenses, he took over the rug company with high expectations. When the business failed and went into bankruptcy, he tried his hand at gambling, bankrolling his efforts with marijuana sales, according to authorities.

At the time of the assassination, Chagra had an alibi. He was in Las Vegas, where he had earned a reputation as a high-rolling gambler who thought nothing about handing out $10,000 tips. Because investigators considered him the prime suspect, their efforts focused on individuals he might have hired to carry out the assassination.

*   *   *

Two days after the assassin's bullet killed Judge Wood, Don Moore and I were summoned to Director William H. Webster's office. We referred to him as Judge Webster because he had left a position on the U.S. Court of Appeals for the Eighth Circuit to become the FBI Director. The man he replaced was Acting Director James B. Adams, a career FBI special agent who became an associate director to Judge Webster once he stepped down from the director's position.

We had no idea why we had been summoned to Director Webster's office. Also present in the office was Lee Coldwell, the executive assistant director. Judge Webster had been a straight-laced, fact-finding judge. He did not want to hear you state, "I think" or "I believe." He wanted facts. If you did not have the facts, then you'd better go get the facts. He taught us lessons on how to sit down and describe an investigation.

Judge Webster quickly let Don Moore and me know that he had met with Attorney General Griffin Bell. He and Bell had received a telephone call from Chief Judge Sessions from San Antonio and the Chief Judge, who later became the director of the FBI, was not happy with the way the investigation was going in San Antonio. I proceeded to tell those present that the shooting had just occurred and the San Antonio office . . . I was stopped in midsentence.

"Ingram, you are going to San Antonio," said Judge Webster. "You have a track record of organizing special investigations and finding witnesses and finding solutions."

He was still talking and I was thinking that those were indeed compliments, especially coming from the Director, when his words stopped me cold.

"Call your wife," Judge Webster continued. "Tell her your plans. Tell her to pack your bags and we will have an agent pick up your luggage. Be sure to tell her to pack sufficient clothing for a long stay in San Antonio. Your plane transportation has already been made. You will depart at [he gave me the exact time] today. Your luggage will be shipped to the FBI office in San Antonio. You should see Judge Sessions because we have already told him you are being dispatched to head up this investigation. You will tell the SAC Tony Morrow that he is in charge of the investigation surrounding the San Antonio office, but you are in charge of the killing of John. H. Wood."

There wasn't a lot of give and take in that meeting. It was like walking into a room to see a machinegun demonstration take place. Rat-tat-tat-ta-tat. Judge Webster didn't mince words. I was called into the office to receive his orders face-to-face, not to debate tactics in the investigation. I felt good in some respects because, after all, I knew I had the support of Judge Webster and my good friend Lee Coldwell because I'd had some trying times over the past four years. After all that sank in, Judge Webster continued: "Ingram, I know you have asked me to be transferred out of Washington and you'd like to go to Jackson, Mississippi, but that

156

can't be done. You go to San Antonio and then we'll discuss transfer out of Washington when you return."

I thanked the judge. I thanked Lee Coldwell. Then I walked out with Don Moore. Outside the office, Don, whom I truly loved and called Big Daddy, said, "Jimbo, you've done it again. All those years of working under Roy Moore has rubbed off on you and now you have to live up to that reputation."

I departed that day and landed in San Antonio, where I was met by an FBI agent who took me to the office to be briefed. I immediately made plans to contact Chief Judge Sessions to tell him that we were going to get the job done.

Of course, the news media already had been alerted there was a new man in town. The San Antonio newspapers put my picture and background on the front pages and made it clear the FBI was pulling all stops by having a person from Washington come to San Antonio to "solve this case."

First on my list was to arrange a meeting with the Texas Rangers to tell them of our plans. I assured them we wanted to work together on the case because it was a matter that had received the highest priority at all levels of government. Then I met with the chief of police in San Antonio and his assistants. We talked about where we were and where we needed to go.

Almost immediately I was contacted by a group called Committee of Justice. This group of business executives already had received pledges for a $100,000 reward for information leading to the conviction of Judge Wood's assassin. They asked for my input before making an announcement at the St. Anthony Hotel that San Antonio citizens were joining law enforcement, not only to express outrage over the killing, but to express the belief that amount would result in people coming forward with information. Sam Millsap was the leader of this group and I met with him several times during our investigation. I was authorized by the FBI to announce that an additional $25,000 would be added to the reward by the federal government. In 1979, $125,000 was lot of money for a reward, so we expected to receive some tips.

I already had made the decision that we would have agents on duty 24 hours a day. That meant we wanted to select only those agents who were willing to work seven days a week. I provided the news media with a telephone number—I remember it to this day—

and let it be known that we would man that telephone 24 hours a day for any calls regarding the judge's assassination. We also set up a special mailbox for people who wanted to mail us information about the shooting.

I knew full well there would be a certain element that would use the telephone number or mailbox to incriminate people they did not like who had nothing to do with the case, but we had plenty of experience with tips of that nature. We had to have something to go on. Anytime you have a case in which an individual used a rifle to assassinate someone from a distance, you seldom have a witness who has seen the attack.

I set up a command post and named Herb Hawkins as my operations manager. He was energetic and enthusiastic and he knew how to get the job done. We brought in agents from other field offices to conduct the investigations. We knew that sooner or later we would be successful.

Almost immediately we started receiving tips.

Most of those early tips identified the Bandito Motorcycle Gang. They were involved in drug smuggling and as some informants stated they had every reason to see Judge Wood put out of commission. But those tips always went down a dead-end street.

My job was to get the special investigation going, organize the manpower, get it clocking 24 hours a day and work with the Texas Rangers, San Antonio Police Department and federal and state agencies, which I did. Once I did all that I was asked to do, I was called back to Washington to take on a new assignment in another city, just as Director Webster had promised. Jack Lawn took my place as the new SAC in San Antonio and he hit the ground running. Oliver "Buck" Revell took my place as assistant director of the criminal division in Washington.

Meanwhile, Jimmy Chagra's drug trafficking trial was moved to Austin, where Judge Sessions, wearing a bulletproof vest, presided. Sessions had delivered the eulogy at Judge Wood's funeral and served as a pallbearer. The jury took less than two hours to find Chagra guilty of every charge in the indictment. Sessions released Chagra on $1 million bond and he quickly jumped bail and disappeared, possibly to South America. Agents figured he eventually would return to Las Vegas—and he did. He was apprehended, sentenced to thirty years without parole by Judge

Sessions, and assigned to the Federal Penitentiary at Leavenworth, Kansas.

The break in the WOODMUR case actually came from the Kansas City field office, with Special Agent Floyd Clarke pushing the case there and Buck Revell spearheading the Washington effort. As it happened, Kansas City agents developed an informant in the Federal Penitentiary at Leavenworth, where a new suspect, Charles Harrelson (actor Woody Harrelson's father), had recently served time. Once the informant linked Harrelson, who was then out on parole, and Chagra to the murder of Judge Wood, the FBI wasted no time installing electronic listening devices inside the prison to record Chagra's conversations. They also began an investigation of Harrelson, who, by then, already was back in custody on unrelated charges.

It took four years for justice to be realized in Judge Wood's assassination. Even then, the jury acquitted Jimmy Chagra of hiring the killer, but found him guilty of two lesser charges— conspiring to smuggle drugs and obstructing justice. Chagra was sentenced to fifteen years in prison, to be added onto the thirty-five-year sentence he already was serving.

Chagra's conviction on lesser charges came as a surprise to many, especially after Kathryn Wood, the judge's widow, read in court a hand-written letter addressed to her from Chagra's wife, Elizabeth. In the letter she apologized for her role in the assassination, saying "I was in the kitchen cooking fried chicken when my husband came home and said, 'I'm going to kill Judge Wood." The letter also indicated that Elizabeth had delivered a bag of money to Las Vegas, "the payoff for your husband's murder."

As the triggerman, Harrelson was sentenced to two life sentences to run consecutively after he completed the seventy years he already was facing. Woody Harrelson, who portrayed a psychopath in Oliver Stone's film, *Natural Born Killers*, spent not only a lot of money but a lot of time attempting to get his father released from prison. But Harrelson died of a heart attack in his prison cell in 2007 at the age of 69. Chagra died of cancer the following year.

Through news accounts, Harrelson stated that he intended to write his memoirs some day and reveal some of the killings committed by him. It will be interesting to see if Woody Harrelson and his family allow the memoirs to be published. Everyone in the judicial community was extremely pleased with Harrelson's conviction, in particular the Committee for Justice, the membership of which stood tall at a time when San Antonio needed members of the community to come forth.

*　*　*

Just before I departed Washington, D.C., for Chicago, Judge Webster summoned me to his office. We sat down and had a delightful chat of our time together. He told me his daughter and her husband had just moved to a suburb of Chicago, Hillsdale. He and Mrs. Webster would be traveling often to Chicago to visit them. He had already informed his daughter of my impending transfer in the event she needed immediate help from me.

I was delighted and one of the first things I did when I reached Chicago was to contact his daughter and son-in-law to provide them with the necessary telephone numbers.

Before leaving Washington, I went to the U.S. Capitol to inform Mississippi Senator James Eastland of my transfer.

"Ingram, you should have gone to Mississippi," he said.

"Senator, that was where I wanted to go, but that was just not in the cards."

"I understand. We will be chatting."

I then went by the Department of Justice to pay my respects to Ben Civiletti, but he was away on business. I wanted to let him know how appreciative I was of his handling of my case. I looked back on my days in Washington with pride because we celebrated our 200th birthday in 1976 without any bombings, or any terrorist acts. Across the country America was safe.

After five years in Washington, D.C., I was extremely pleased to depart and start a new life in Chicago, where the FBI office had always been regarded as one of the premier offices because of its history of providing some of the finest work in criminal and domestic intelligence. Upon my arrival in Chicago, I called upon Dick Held, former SAC in Chicago, as he knew just about everyone in Chicago. I also called on former Attorney General Ed Levi. I had met Mr. Levi while in Washington and after his retirement from government service he returned to Chicago. He was a brilliant man. He and Judge Webster had an excellent relationship. I also renewed my acquaintance with all the agents working the FALN case in Chicago because I had followed their work when I was in New York.

Chicago is the heartland, with every ethnic group imaginable residing and working there. Chicago was like the rest of the country in the sense that there were long lines for gasoline. Economic problems during President Jimmy Carter's administration had pushed mortgage rates to 17 and 19 percent and people were sickened with the way things were going.

EDITOR'S NOTE

By late 1978 the world's hot spot was Iran, where Mohammad Shah Pahlavi, better known as the Shah of Iran, had held onto power since 1941. Challenging his authority to lead Iran were Islamic clerics, led by the Ayatollah Khomeini, the spiritual leader of a rapidly building Islamic revolution that felt the Shah had compromised Islamic tradition by a series of radical reforms that included land redistribution and voting rights for women.

In early September 1978, the Shah's army fired on a group of demonstrators, killing and wounding thousands. As demonstrations spread throughout Iran—and as the middle class stepped away from the Shah because of a belief that his programs benefited only the elite—it became apparent to U.S. officials that the Shah's days as Iran's ruler were numbered. U.S. military planners sprang into action to develop contingency plans to deal with the sudden fall of the Shah and the possibility of Americans being taken hostage by militant Islamic revolutionaries.

That month the Special Operations division of the U.S. Army at Fort Bragg, North Carolina, requested the assistance of the FBI for a top-secret training mission. For FBI Director William H. Webster there was only one person in the bureau capable of providing the assistance necessary—Jim Ingram, who recently had been transferred to the Washington, D.C. office, where he was put in charge of anti-terrorism activities. By that point in his career he was the FBI's leading expert on terrorism. Drawing agents from the Charlotte and Raleigh, North Carolina, and Richmond, Virginia, offices, he put together an anti-terrorism team to work with the special operations command.

As opposition to the Shah escalated in Iran, Texas-based Electric Data System (later the company name would be changed

161

to Hewlett-Packard) evacuated most of its 100 American employees and more than 200 dependents from Tehran in December 1978, leaving behind only a handful of workers. Two of them were subsequently taken prisoner in late December and incarcerated in an Iranian prison where political dissidents were routinely held. The United States had worked closely with the Shah for years, but finding a solution for the release of the two Americans was problematic.

Iran was in the midst of a revolution. The Shah couldn't release the men because it might inflame Islamist religious leaders and topple his government.

Enter Texas billionaire Ross Perot, owner of EDS. After being told there was nothing the U.S. government could do to assist his employees, he devised a plan to send a group of highly trained operatives into Iran to rescue them. He asked retired U.S. Army Colonel Bull Simons, an expert on Special Forces operations, to recruit and train half a dozen men, including a retired Green Beret officer, and Ross Perot, for a top secret incursion into Iran to attempt a rescue attempt. That much is public record. Most of the EDS employees selected for the mission were veterans who had served on the battlefields of Vietnam.

Although the exact nature of Jim Ingram's training activities with the Special Forces remains top secret, it coincided with the turmoil in Iran and almost certainly had to do with providing Special Forces personnel the information they needed to conduct successful clandestine operations inside Iran.

Once training was completed and arrangements were completed, Perot and his raiders flew to Tehran weeks before their rescue attempt and quickly blended into the city, not a difficult undertaking because at that point, at least, the festering Iranian revolution was directed at the Shah, not the United States.

For that reason, Iranian authorities paid little attention to the arrival of new EDS employees. The idea was to perform a special operations-style jailbreak to rescue the two men, but before the plan could be put into effect Iranian revolutionaries stormed the prison and freed 11,000 inmates, many of them political dissidents. Included were the two EDS employees who quickly made contact with Perot's raiders once they left the prison. The men were driven to the Turkish border, where they were able to catch a flight back to the United States.

Within weeks, on January 16, 1979, the Shah fled from Iran, allowing Ayatollah Khomeini to seize power. After visiting several countries, he came to the United States to receive medical treatment for cancer. His first stop was New York City, where he attracted unwanted attention from protestors. Iranian militants responded to his entry into the United States by storming the American Embassy in Tehran and seizing 52 American hostages.

Ordinarily, the Shah would have received Secret Service protection upon his arrival in the United States, but President Jimmy Carter felt that would send the wrong signal to the Ayatollah Khomeini. He did not want to do anything that would bring harm to the hostages. Instead, Carter asked the FBI to provide protection to the Shah until such time as he could be turned over to the U.S. Air Force.

Accordingly, Jim Ingram's old friend, Oliver "Buck" Revell was put in charge of safely delivering the Shah and his wife to the Air Force base in San Antonio, where his cancer treatments could begin. The entourage was transported to Texas on two 707s, accompanied by a team of FBI agents. Shortly before the Shah's arrival an entire wing of the base hospital was cleared of patients so that security could be provided during his medical treatments. Everyone knew the Shah was marked for death by the militants.

Jim Ingram spent most of his life solving mysteries for the FBI. In this case he left a mystery for me to solve because nowhere in his interview tapes is there ever a mention of the Shah of Iran. The subject arose by accident one day while we were talking about a wide range of subjects while sitting in a car in a Walgreen's parking lot. I asked him what he knew about the Shah's visit to Jackson. For a second he looked shocked, but then he smiled and quickly recovered and said, "I'll check into that and get back to you," a twinkle in his eye. He never did, of course.

At the time of the Shah's arrival in America, I was a reporter for the *Jackson Daily News*, an afternoon newspaper in Mississippi. I received a tip that the Shah was living in a safe house in Jackson, presumably to receive treatment for his cancer. As I began my investigation, my editor, Jimmy Ward, a frequent source of information to the FBI, called me into his office and closed the door and told me that the FBI had contacted him about my inquiries and asked the newspaper not to report the Shah's arrival in Jackson for national security reasons and to protect the hostages in Iran. Unhappy to lose a story of international interest, I did understand the security issues involved and I agreed not to pursue the story. I did not want to be the cause of hostage executions in Iran. The Shah came and went without anyone ever knowing about his visit.

In September 1978, a Commander at Fort Bragg, North Carolina, sent FBI Director William H. Webster a letter, obtained by me with the assistance of the FBI, thanking the director for his support of the joint training exercise that the Special Operations Command undertook with the FBI at Fort Bragg. Wrote the commander: "My special thanks go to Mr. James O. Ingram, who was most instrumental in coordinating the exercise with my staff and who did so enthusiastically and effectively . . . The results of the exercise were extremely encouraging and we intend to repeat it on a quarterly basis hoping that we will be given the same assistance as during the first exercise. I consider our mutual and continued cooperation absolutely essential to the successful accomplishment of our mission and hope that it will become even closer in the future."

In 1979, when the Shah came to Jackson, I had no idea who Jim Ingram was. Now I can see how he might have pulled the strings from Washington, D.C. or later Chicago that brought the Shah to a city that Ingram loved and knew so well. Never in a million years would anyone ever suspect that the Shah was in hiding in the "Magnolia State."

—**James L. Dickerson**

The lives of 52 American hostages hung in the balance for the duration of the Iranian crisis. This began a long, bitter battle between the United States and the Iranian government. Iran shut off oil to the United States and Ayatollah Ruhollah Khomeini issued dire threats to the United States if the shah was not handed over to them. The ayatollah also asked the Iranian nation to mobilize against the United States. This is interesting because more than three decades later we are going through the same situation with Iran. Some things never seem to change.

In early 1980, President Carter severed all ties with Iran. All envoys in the United States representing Iran were told to leave. The president also put a halt on visas. During this period, as the Special Agent in Charge in Chicago, I was told to close the Iranian mission in Chicago, which I did.

164

In 1980, a rescue effort was attempted to free the hostages in Iran and it failed. The president spent the next month defending his decision to attempt to rescue the hostages.

In July of that year, the Shah of Iran passed away, but it changed nothing as far as the hostages were concerned. We were constantly on standby because you never knew if war was imminent. Then in early January 1981, the United States gave Iran a January 16 deadline and, as we all know, Ronald Reagan was president by then, and the hostages were all immediately released and set free. This ended a sad note in history, but it was important because the FBI was certainly in the middle of it all.

* * *

On June 10, 1980, United Airlines President Percy Wood accepted a package sent to him at his home in Lake Forest, Illinois. On the package were stamps commemorating playwright Eugene O'Neill, a known supporter of anarchists. The package contained a book titled *Ice Brothers,* written by Sloan Wilson, also the author of *The Man in the Gray Flannel Suit.* With the book was a note that said, "You will find it of great social significance."

Unfortunately, the book was hollowed out to make room for a bomb. When Mr. Wood opened the book, the package detonated and severely wounded Mr. Wood. However, he did recover. We knew, based on other package bombs that had been delivered around Chicago, that we still had an active group of terrorists. This particular bomb was later proved to be the work of Theodore "Ted" Kaczynski, the so-called "Unabomber," but we didn't know that at the time.

Three previous incidents involving bombs in the Chicago area already had been linked to the same unidentified suspect. The first involved a package mailed to the University of Illinois at the Chicago campus; it was returned unopened to the return address at Northwestern University and exploded, injuring a campus police officer. The second explosion occurred a year later at Northwestern when a cigar box exploded injuring a student. The third caused a fire in the cargo hold of an American Airlines flight from Chicago to Washington, D.C., prompting an emergency landing. No one was injured, but the incident could have been disastrous. More than a dozen bombings followed. The evidence we sent to the FBI Laboratory indicated that it was the work of the same suspect, but

165

the case was not solved until Ted Kaczynski's brother stepped forward to inform us of his suspicions about his brother.

During that time we also had many active cases involving organized crime. We had one matter in which the Deputy Superintendent of Scotland Yard and his assistant came to Chicago regarding a jewelry heist that had occurred in London. We were able to help them with a solution to that crime.

Seldom did I see a reason to close my doors anytime I conferred with agents, but in late 1980 I had a conference that was of such importance that I closed my doors when I was briefed by agents about corruption that was occurring in the Cook County court system, particularly in the courtroom of Judge Wayne Olson.

Tom Sullivan was the U.S. Attorney in Chicago. I enjoyed working with Tom because he was a true professional, a person of integrity who was well respected by his peers in Chicago and also at the U.S. Department of Justice. The discussion with Sullivan resulted in an active investigation of Olson and others around him.

At the beginning of the investigation I called Buck Revell in Washington and told him what we had. I told him we wanted to put a concealed microphone in the chambers of Judge Olson. That was an unprecedented request because never in the history of the FBI had the agency targeted judges with listening devices.

Revell told me that would be a hard sell with Director Webster, himself a former judge. Standing in the way was a public firestorm over ABSCAM, an undercover sting operation instigated by the FBI to investigate corruption among elected officials at the local, state and national level. Implicated in the investigation were a U.S. senator and several congressmen who accepted bribes from FBI undercover agents masquerading as wealthy Arab sheiks. The undercover agents had approached the officials and offered cash or stock in exchange for gambling licenses.

"The fires of indignation from our ABSCAM case were still burning brightly, and Webster would not easily accept that we should invade the sanctity of a judge's chamber," wrote Revell in his memoir, *A G-Man's Journal.* "Jim understood this, and we discussed a strategy to put forward our best argument to the Director and the Department of Justice."

Together we developed a plan whereby I would ask Tom Sullivan to contact Assistant Attorney General Phil Heymann, thus

166

opening the way for Revell to meet with Heymann to make certain that he was on board before we approached Director Webster. Revell felt pretty confident about Heymann because he had once commented that he would go after the President if that is where an investigation led. As we had hoped, Heymann and his staff said they would back our efforts as long as FBI agents maintained full control of the microphone and only activated it when Judge Olson was in private meetings with known suspects. That was no problem because we already had solved the technical difficulties associated with the case.

When Revell presented the proposal to Director Webster, he responded as we had expected. Wrote Revell: "To him, the very thought of placing a bug in a judge's chamber was repugnant. In response we went through the history of corruption in Chicago courts, and why no other investigative technique would work. We pointed out the type of criminal who was getting off. This seemed to sway Webster's mind, but he still withheld his approval until he could give the case further study."

Meanwhile, Webster came to Chicago and met with us, explaining the situation that we were getting into. Revell and I both understood that we personally would be held responsible if something went wrong in the investigation we named GREYLORD. At that time the state's attorney of Cook County was Richard Daley, who went on to become mayor. We asked the director if we could brief Daley on the secret operation and he gave his approval. Daley was just outstanding. He made available a young man from his office to work as the undercover agent. This young man was Terry Hake and he handled his duties superbly.

A few days after he returned to Washington, Director Webster approved the application. Agents installed a microphone in Judge Olson's desk and within a matter of days, examples of crime and corruption spewed forth like a geyser. It ended up being a huge success, with convictions of 87 court personnel and attorneys and thirteen judges. We were all very relieved that we were able to do this investigation under complete secrecy with the aid of Daley and his staff and Tom Sullivan and his staff. It was truly one of the finest works of the FBI.

*   *   *

One of things that pleased me about my Chicago assignment was that it allowed me to again work with one of my favorite agents, Rick Hahn. He knew more about the FALN than anyone else. The FALN, which was founded in the 1960s, was a paramilitary organization that used bombs against innocent civilians to draw attention to United States government efforts to discourage the independence movement in Puerto Rico. The group was classified as a terrorist organization by the FBI.

Hahn had worked on the bombing cases with me when we were both assigned to the New York field office. Before returning to Chicago, he worked in San Juan to assist agents in attempting to stem the tide of terrorist bombers. In the 1970s, Rick was given the task of reviewing the entire spectrum of terrorist bombings attributed to FALN in an effort to come up with a plan to help agents in the field. Rick was a pretty smart fellow who had attended Dartmouth. As a result of his suggestions, the FBI was able to implement a plan in field offices around the country.

On March 18, 1980, armed terrorists shouting Puerto Rican nationalist slogans invaded the Carter-Mondale campaign headquarters on Dearborn Avenue in Chicago. Six armed people were involved and one of the terrorists identified was FBI fugitive Carlos Alberto Torres, who was on top of the FBI most wanted fugitive list because of the bombing of the New York tavern. None of the campaign workers were tied up or injured.

Three weeks later we received a big break. After observing a suspicious van in a residential neighborhood adjacent to North-western University, the Evanston, Illinois police approached the van, prompting the male driver to flee, leaving his passengers stranded inside. The good work of the police resulted in the arrest of eleven people, six men and five women. Some of the suspects wore jogging suits.

Inside the van were several ski masks and a number of firearms. Among those arrested were Carlos Torres and his wife Maria. Our agents immediately went to the scene to assist the police. There is no doubt that the arrests prevented other terrorist acts. We had received information that the FALN had a plan to disrupt the Republican and Democrat conventions during the summer.

In February 1981 U.S. District Judge Thomas McMillen sentenced Torres, the reputed ringleader, to 70 years in prison. The judge said that if he had been empowered by Congress to impose the death penalty he would have done so. Another member of the group was sentenced to 60 years in prison. Each member of the group was convicted and sentenced. During the sentencing stage, about fifty supporters of the group marched outside the federal building in Dearborn. This was a good day for the government as we were able to put in prison several members of the FALN to stem the tide of terrorist acts.

Despite the seriousness of the crimes taking place in Chicago during my years there, there were moments of enjoyment. I had the good fortune of being asked to join a small luncheon group that met weekly with Bill Wrigley of the Wrigley Company, Abe Pritzker of the Hyatt Corp., Christie Hefner of Playboy, and others. I also had the pleasure of getting to know Coach George Halas, one of the original founders of the NFL, owner and coach of the Chicago Bears. Coach Halas became a dear friend as a result of our encounters.

Jim Ingram, left, offering firearm instruction

12

CODE NAME COINTELPRO

The civil rights division of the Justice Department did one thing for me that I will always appreciate. They assigned attorney Gordon W. Daiger to represent me and the other two agents in the depositions that we had to give to the American Civil Liberties Union (ACLU). On our first meeting, Gordon, who knew of my personal plight, asked, "How can you be so friendly and so outgoing, with everything hanging over your head?"

"Gordon, it will all work out," I responded. "I have faith because I know I have done nothing to violate the Bureau's rules in the ACLU lawsuit, nor did I do anything in the GAO audit."

Gordon looked at me as if to say, "Do I believe this?"

As the case progressed, we spent hours and hours together. One night after a long session with ACLU lawyers and a deposition where he had fought vigorously with ACLU attorneys, Gordon looked up from his paperwork and said something that astonished me.

"We're going to beat the bastards."

I said, "Gordon, that doesn't sound like you."

"Well, I can be as mean spirited as they can."

"Gordon, that still does not sound like you."

"Let me handle the mean spirit," Gordon said. "You continue your nice Mississippi ways."

I'll always remember that.

* * *

It should be noted that during the 1970s, and certainly in the 1960s, I had worked well with the civil rights division of the U.S. Justice Department, and in the 2000s, especially 2005 to 2008, I worked very closely with them on some of the old murder cases that we successfully brought to trial. More about that later.

The U.S. Justice Department is unique to those prosecutorial agencies in other countries charged with enforcing the laws. The criminal division investigates alleged violations of criminal laws and prosecutes those who violate those laws, while the civil rights division investigates alleged civil rights violations established by the law. The FBI works with both divisions, by gathering and providing investigative information that assists in prosecutions. For that reason, FBI personnel in one division sometimes come under investigation by personnel in the other division for allegedly breaking laws established to protect the rights of individuals under investigation for illegal activities.

So it was with me. I was under investigation for approving the use of surreptitious entry in cases involving domestic terrorism. I maintained my innocence, but that was beside the point. I was still under investigation. Others also came under investigation. In 1978 a federal grand jury indicted former Acting Director Patrick Grey, Acting Associate Director Mark Felt, and former Assistant Director Ed Miller for approving the use of surreptitious entry. This was in connection with the FBI's investigation of the Weather Underground fugitives who allegedly had committed bombings from the West Coast to the East Coast.

Wally LaPrade, an assistant director, was indicted as a co-conspirator. Wally was my very good friend and still is today. Wally appeared before the grand jury three times, trying to explain the system and what he did and what he did not do. Wally was an honest, independent individual, who spoke his mind publicly, making Attorney General Griffin Bell livid.

As I recall, Wally let his feelings be known about President Jimmy Carter and others, and he challenged Attorney General Bell to a debate on wiretaps. Wally had stated to me that they were looking for perjury charges. Wally and I never talked during this period because we wanted to be able to say we had not discussed anything about the grand jury with each other. My attorney made it clear to the Justice Department attorneys that if they forced me to appear before the grand jury I would invoke the Fifth Amendment. I knew what they were looking for and I knew I was innocent. I was not about to play their game.

In November 1980, Gray, Felt and Miller were convicted in federal court in Washington, D.C. of conspiring to violate the civil rights of Weatherman fugitives. I personally liked Attorney General Bell and he, in my opinion, was the very best of Carter's cabinet. After the conviction, he publicly stated he was not happy with the results because he knew the black bag jobs, as they were called, had been carried out for years by the government and former presidents, and former attorneys general had known about those activities and had not sought prosecutions.

In 1981, President Reagan pardoned the three former FBI executives. Later, as we well know, Mark Felt publicly admitted that he was Deep Throat and had furnished classified information of the FBI's investigation of Watergate to the *Washington Post*. To make a point, when I refused to take a polygraph because I was innocent, I have often thought of my friend Buck Revell, a former Oklahoman who could do it all at the bureau.

I knew that Buck was a man of integrity because I served with him on a career promotion board of which Buck was chairman. We had five people on the board. Deputy Assistant Director Bill Bailey, Nick Stains, Deputy Assistant Director Bill Krieger, Buck, and myself. This was a very important board because we made recommendation to the FBI directors for those individuals who had the experience and were qualified to be future executives of the FBI. We all agreed at the outset that the Bureau needed to promote the best qualified for the field operations and we must find the best qualified minorities. We had very few female agents at that time, so none had been in the bureau long enough to be considered. Regarding Buck and polygraphs, some allegations were made against him and he took a polygraph examination and the first reading was not a good one. He took a second examination and it took Buck quite some time to prove his innocence over a matter.

*   *   *

My nightmare with the ACLU lawsuit was still far from over, but the General Accounting Office (GAO) ordeal came to an abrupt halt in February 1980. After three years of investigation by the Justice Department, Ben Civiletti, deputy attorney general, advised the FBI director that the inquiry regarding myself for alleged non-disclosure of information to the GAO could be deemed to be purely administrative by the bureau. Mr. Civiletti indicated that my prosecution had been declined and they were going to close their file.

All that is interesting in that in my first meeting with Mr. Civilette, whom I found to be a very reasonable gentleman, in Jim Adams's office on a matter having nothing to do with my investigation, he was cold and did not communicate with me during that meeting. At subsequent meetings, he warmed up and I

173

think that in his own mind, he must have been thinking that perhaps Ingram as not as bad as he was touted to be.

Working for Jim Adams was a complete joy. I went to the White house situation room with him on occasion. I also went to CIA headquarters with him, where I first met CIA Director George H. Bush, who later became our vice president and then our president. I'll always remember when we walked into Director Bush's office, as he got up to greet us, how tall and straight he was and how he carried himself extremely well.

I will always be grateful for the support of Jim Adams, Don Moore, and particularly Lee Coldwell, who pushed the department for an answer on me. Coldwell had an excellent relationship with the attorney general and Civiletti and he urged the attorney general's office to reach a decision on me because three years was enough. For three years I had been under a strain and I know that was when I started losing my hair.

One day I received a letter from FBI Director William H. Webster notifying me that the Justice Department had declined prosecution of me for nondisclosure of information to GAO regarding the bureau's COINTELPRO programs related to the Weathermen and other radical groups.

In his letter, Webster wrote: "I have reviewed the results of our inquiry and discussed this matter personally with you. The inquiry revealed that you did, in fact, participate in the failure of the FBI to disclose entries in an investigative matter to GAO. Although you were following instructions from a superior, you are culpable to the extent that you took part in an effort to withhold information from GAO. Your participation in acts that resulted in the FBI's not making a full and timely disclosure of surreptitious entries was a serious matter, and you should have been aware that the result of your action would be a misrepresentation to GAO. I believe I have adequately expressed to you personally my concern for what I consider an aberration of your otherwise superior performance and dedication to duty. . . I have decided, in view of your superior work performance over the past three and one-half years and your candid cooperation in this inquiry, that this letter and my discussion with you adequately dealt with this lapse in your otherwise usual good judgment. Accordingly, no further administrative action is contemplated."

174

EDITOR'S NOTE

FBI agent Bill Stokes, with whom Jim Ingram worked on cold-case, civil rights era murders in the mid-2000s, explains Jim's troubles with COINTELPRO this way: "The biggest thorn in his side was COINTELPRO. There is an old saying in the FBI. If you are working, you are in trouble. If you are not working, you are not in trouble. There are three categories of cases. No cases. Kinda' cases. And big cases. Jim was always a big case guy—a long ball hitter. He didn't hit singles. He took the ball out of the park."

—James L. Dickerson

*   *   *

In early October 1981, I began to experience chest pain, palpitations, and shortness of breath. I went to my doctor for a checkup and he put me in Billings Hospital at the University of Chicago for tests under the direction of a noted cardiologist. They kept me in the hospital for a week. The diagnosis was that I had suffered a mitral valve prolapse, which in layman's terms meant that my heart's mitral valve was not closing tightly enough.

I returned to work on October 13 with the realization that mine was not the type of job where you could kick back and coast into retirement. The more years you put into the Bureau, the more valuable your knowledge and experience becomes to the Bureau— and the more demands it makes of you. In many respects, I worked harder as the Special Agent in Charge of the Chicago office than I did as a young agent.

Looking ahead to the holidays, I filed for personal leave that would take place between November 30, 1981, and December 23, 1981. A mitral valve prolapse was reason enough to take some time off to reexamine one's life, but there were other considerations. Ever since we moved to Chicago, Marie and I had felt the emotional draw to Mississippi and our grown sons. At our ages, we were both approaching the age of fifty, we were eager for stability in our private lives. The prospect of entering our senior years apart from our sons and grandchildren was not appealing. We returned to Mississippi whenever possible, but those visits did not occur with nearly the frequency we desired.

On November 10, 1981, the day after requesting personal leave, I requested retirement from the FBI, effective January 22, 1982. After twenty-nine years with the FBI, I decided it was time to step down. In a letter to FBI Director William H. Webster, I reminded him that I had discussed my plans with the director during his November business trip to Chicago.

In my letter I wrote: "I reluctantly must close my career in the FBI. I consider myself fortunate to have had the opportunity to serve you as a Deputy in the Criminal Investigative Division in Washington, D.C., when you became director of the FBI, and I was deeply honored upon your appointment of me as Special Agent in Charge of the Chicago Division. Your dedication and skillful leadership have restored the FBI to a great institution. I am proud to have had an opportunity to be with the FBI under your guidance. Judge, I will always be available to you and to this organization."

Director Webster responded with a "Dear Jim" letter dated December 18, 1981. He accepted my resignation with regret and wrote: "From the time I first came to the Bureau almost four years ago, you have been a standout member of my team. No assignment has failed to receive your full and energetic attention and you have been a shining example to others. I recall your skill at crisis management at Headquarters and your foundation blocks for the John Wood assassination, one of the most important and difficult undertakings in recent times. I watched you carry out your responsibilities during a period of personal stress in which the conduct of many Agents had been questioned on the basis of 20/20 hindsight. You never wavered in your full devotion to the Bureau and our mission. In Chicago you made us all proud. The work of the men and women in your office is outstanding . . . Were it not for your earnest desire to return to Jackson to be with your children and grandchildren I would have tried to persuade you to make yourself available for increased responsibilities back here. So I shall not try, but instead wish you all continued success and happiness and Godspeed in the years ahead."

After 29 years as an FBI special agent, I was leaving the FBI with mixed feelings—there had been some rough years mixed in with the good years—but I always believed in the Bureau and its mission, and I will always be proud of my years of service. However, Marie and I had Mississippi on our mind—and there was nothing left to do but to make our relocation a reality. Our three sons had never left Mississippi. They all remained in the state, where they obtained degrees from the University of Mississippi—two in law, the other in business.

It was with a great sense of relief that we knew we had experienced our last relocation. However, our transition was not as smooth as we had hoped. My personal leave request, which was approved by the appropriate channels, allowed us to travel to Mississippi to prepare for our transition to civilian life.

Unfortunately, more than a month after approval for the leave was granted, it was rescinded by the Personnel Section of the U.S. General Services Administration in a memorandum to Director Webster. The memo stated that I would be unable to take the leave because of "urgent official business" that required my presence in Chicago. Among the items on the list that required my presence in Chicago were a luncheon to honor law enforcement officials from around the city, an FBI National Training Academy meeting, an organized crime regional conference, planning for an FBI raid associated with an undercover investigation of organized crime elements in Chicago, and the monitoring of two agents who had been wounded in a firearms incident.

All of those items were important functions of a SAC, but I couldn't help wonder if they would have been better handled by the individual selected to replace me, for continuity, if nothing else, going into the New Year.

I didn't think much about it at the time, but my co-author could not help but wonder under what authority the U.S. General Services Administration would have advance notice of a top secret organized crime raid in Chicago. If they knew, who else knew?

Marie and I would have liked to have gone home between Thanksgiving and Christmas to visit with family and prepare for our relocation, but I didn't make a big deal of the leave rejection. I did what I'd always done. I did my job as I had done for 29 years—without complaint. Only by this time I had my sights set on

Mississippi. The only unresolved business I had regarding my long association with the FBI was the lawsuit filed by the ACLU. In some ways it hung over our heads like the Sword of Damocles, a reminder that with great success and satisfaction there also can come great peril and anxiety.

Jim Ingram, left with Mississippi Gov. Kirk Fordice

13

MISSISSIPPI ON MY MIND

EDITOR'S NOTE

With his FBI career seemingly wrapped up, Jim Ingram returned to Mississippi with his wife, Marie, with the hopes of settling into a quiet position in the private sector. Other agents had successfully made the transition from government service to the business world. Jim hoped to follow in their footsteps. He was well known in Mississippi, but very few people knew that he was the bureau's top expert on terrorism at the time of his retirement.

In that sense he led a secret life: On the outside he was an affable individual who laughed easily and often—a man who enjoyed family get-togethers and social events (he served as president of the Jackson Rotary Club and security chief for the International Ballet Competition held each year in Jackson)—but on the inside he was a repository of a vast knowledge of domestic and international terrorism. No one, not even his family, was ever aware of that secret life because Jim did not want them to be burdened by that knowledge.

—James L. Dickerson

My first post-FBI job was with the largest bank in Mississippi, Deposit Guaranty Bank, where I went to work as senior vice-president of security. They had branches all over the state, plus in Louisiana and other locations. It was interesting in that I reported to the chairman of the board and the president, so I had a free run of the matters that I wanted to investigate and there was no shortage of material—thefts, embezzlements, bank robberies, assaults of employees, as well as the death of one of the presidents of a branch office during a bank robbery.

All during this time it was necessary for me to listen to the trials and tribulations of employees. They really had not had an outlet over the years for employees to come forward and confidentially explain what they felt was a grievance or a personal problem that existed in their lives.

Today there is a federal law that provides that when a police officer is involved in a domestic dispute with his wife or others, there is a remedy to have his right to carry a firearm removed. In the days when I worked for the bank that remedy did not exist. I had an employee that came forward with a complaint that a police officer had inflicted bodily harm against her and she was trying to get away from him. I questioned whether I should get involved, but I talked to the man and he let me know that it was none of my business. I'd better mind my own business, he said, or he would continue doing what he desired with that woman.

I told him she was an employee of the bank and she had come to me expressing fear of him. I advised him I would go to his chief if necessary. He said his chief certainly would be on his side.

"Well, I know your chief and I don't think so."

I asked him once again to stop his abusive behavior. He made it clear he would not, so I carried it forward until he was told emphatically by his chief to cease and desist—and he did.

I also had an incident where a young teller was sexually harassed by a customer. After listening to the complaint, I went to the home of the individual to ask him not to return to the bank if he was going to sexually harass this person. When I arrived it was his wife who came to the door. I identified myself and asked to speak to her husband, but she made it clear that her husband would not be coming to the door.

"I handle all the banking matters," she said, adding, "What's the problem?"

I told her I'd rather talk to her husband.

"No, you'll talk to me—I run this family. You tell me what you want to tell him."

"Lady, I hate to do this," I said, "but I'm going to tell you that your husband needs to stop going to one of our branches to sexually harass one of our employees."

She gave me one of those looks. About that time, I heard a commotion in another part of the house and I knew the man was home because his car was there.

"Would you repeat that?" she asked.

I told her again.

"Mister, you won't ever have to worry about him going to that branch again attempting to play with one of those little girls. I will handle this matter."

"Thank you ma'am. I appreciate it."

As I was leaving she said, "I appreciate the way you handled this."

"Well, I appreciate you."

We never had any other problems with that man. No one ever saw him again at any of our branches.

We also had sexual harassment by bank employees against other bank employees. Those were handled by me without any difficulty, but it was something that had to be done. I had a very close working relationship with Susan Cain, who worked in human resources. Susan and I had to handle a matter with one of the bank presidents who was harassing a bank employee. I'll always remember how Susan and I worked together to resolve that matter in everyone's favor, except the bank president, who was terminated.

One of the sad aspects of banking is that even though I had conferences all over the state to teach bank employees how to handle themselves during a bank robbery, not everyone followed the script. We had a branch president in Southaven killed in February 1989 when a lone bank robber came into the bank and there were four women and three men in the bank. He held them hostage for a short period. I had always stressed during my bank robbery conferences that if the bank robber came in the bank to hit the floor and stay on the floor. The bank robber only has a few seconds to do what they have to do and get out. They are not going to get down on the floor and try to drag an unwilling body outside the bank.

Randy Lusk, in attempting to save the others from this bank robber, agreed to go outside the bank with him. The Southaven police arrived at the scene. A shoot-out occurred and Randy Lusk was shot and killed along with the bank robber. This hurt me deeply. I spent many hours with Susan Lusk, the wife. The bank did everything possible as well as Tom Long, the chief of police.

The bank robber was an unusual individual. He was from Broken Arrow, Oklahoma, which is a suburb of Tulsa. I wanted to find out more about this individual for the bank's protection. I discovered that this person was a salesman. He would leave his home, travel to other states, case banks and then rob them. Robbing banks was how he made money. He returned to Broken Arrow on weekends to resume his normal life. When he took a hostage, that was one of his few failures. I only bring this up because in the banking business you never know what is going to happen. I investigated almost every type of case imaginable.

During my years with banking, I got more confessions from individuals than I ever thought possible. I had a very close working relationship with the police departments across the state. We worked the bank robberies with the FBI and the police. I would handle the embezzlements until we solved them and then turned them over to authorities. The homicide division of the Jackson Police Department was very kind to me and allowed me to work with them, including the murder of Rose Wright, one of our very popular female employees.

Rose Wright was murdered in her home in northwest Jackson. Her throat was slashed and she was brutally assaulted. We immediately put out a reward and I worked with the police department day and night—and they were outstanding. About three weeks into the investigation, an individual was arrested and subsequently convicted of Rose's murder. She had befriended her killer, a black male, when he came by her home and asked for money. He continued to stop by her home to ask for money, and she always gave it to him. In the end, she ended up paying for her generosity with her life.

I did more interviews and had more confessions during my years at the bank than I ever did at the FBI because when you're dealing with money you're going to have internal thefts and people on the outside of banking attempting to find ways to get money.

*   *   *

Each year the bank hosted an economic conference at the largest auditorium in Jackson, with invitations going out across the state. There were speakers such as David Glass, CEO of Wal-Mart, T. Boone Pickens, the oil magnet, Cokie Roberts, who was with ABC News at the time—these were just some of the individuals who appeared over the years at the conference. I was always asked by the chairman of the board to take care of their needs, pick them up at the airport, take them to dinner, pick them up the next morning—and to make sure all their questions were answered. One of the conference speakers that I will always remember was Cokie Roberts, whom I had watched through the years on television. She was very security conscious.

Coming from Washington, D.C. and before that, New Orleans, Ms. Roberts certainly watched her every move in public. She knew my background and she was appreciative that not only did I walk her to her hotel room, but I checked inside the room and made sure that it was safe and secure. She did not want to go to dinner that night. She had room service. But she asked for my telephone number so she could reach me if she needed my help.

I had already planned to do that because I had done so with the other speakers that came into Jackson, but she was very pleased when I told her I would be available and would remain nearby if she needed help at any hour. She wanted me to come to her room the next morning to walk her to the speaking engagement and to stay with her while she was in Jackson and to get her back to the hotel safely. I will always remember that I was so impressed not only with her presentation, but with the skills she showed in how to handle herself in a difficult situation in a new environment.

In 1991 the bank engaged television personality Art Linkletter from Hollywood to come to Jackson and travel around the state giving motivational speeches. At selected cities in Mississippi invitations were distributed to bank customers and anyone else interested in hearing the motivational speech by Mr. Linkletter. I will always remember how kind he was to me. We enjoyed traveling around the state together. Later, he wrote me a letter in which he said: "I speak at least 75 times a year and have a lot of experience in the ways these events are handled. When I say that your participation was among the very best I have ever experienced it will mean something to you. It was a joy to be with you and to have the support of your very positive personality."

Art Linkletter was well received across the state and was one of the best advertisements for the bank, in my opinion. No other person captured the audience like Art Linkletter. He could have you laughing and at the same time with tears in your eyes because he was so captivating as a speaker and as an individual.

As we traveled about the state, Mr. Linkletter regaled me with stories about his friendships with Gary Cooper, Bob Hope, Lucille

Ball, Charlton Heston and John Wayne. He felt that it was amazing how the group all seemed to think alike and enjoyed each other's company. The one thing that irritated him at one of his performances was when he was supposed to be introduced by a mayor or local dignitary and the person selected to introduce him would start telling jokes and spend too much time on himself.

This irritated him because, after all, he was the star. He said people came to see him, not to hear others go on and on and on. He was correct because we had some individuals who were supposed to introduce him start telling stories and try to be funny.

Art Linkletter, in a very nice way, would turn to the person and say, "I think you've forgotten who the star of the show is," and it always brought the house down. I certainly enjoyed him telling stories on Hollywood because he had a very sad family situation and he discussed those tragedies up to a point and said he had to laugh to keep from crying.

*   *   *

On November 18, 1985, my decade-long lawsuit involving Muhammed Kenyatta and the ACLU finally went to court. I was still working for the bank at the time. The chairman of the board, John Maloney, and Bud Robinson, then president, were very supportive of me during the trial. I let them know that I did not want to embarrass the bank because of the very large black population in Mississippi and that I would tender my resignation prior to the trial so that no stigma would be attached to the bank. They steadfastly refused my offer of resignation and I was very pleased with their support.

During the six-day trial, Roy Moore, Thomas Fitzpatrick and I were represented by U.S. Department of Justice attorneys Teresa A. Scott, Gordon W. Daiger, Mary P. Mitchell, and Peter R. Wubbenhorst of the FBI Legal Counsel Division. Wubbenhorst traveled around the country with Mitchell to gather evidence for the trial. Kenyatta was represented by ACLU attorneys from New York, Philadelphia, and Washington, D.C.

At the trial Kenyatta maintained he was forced to flee the state because he was black and was involved in civil rights activities. His attorneys argued that the three FBI agents named in the lawsuit had violated his civil rights by sending him a forged letter that resulted in him fleeing the state in fear for his life. He alleged this deprived him of free speech, due process of law, and violated his constitutional rights.

We never denied preparing the letter. On the contrary, evidence showed that the letter was prepared under the authority of the COINTELPRO program and was not a product of the fanciful imaginations of Moore, Fitzpatrick and me. On the contrary, it was established bureau policy to use counterintelligence methods for the purpose of preventing violence.

Our defense team introduced evidence that Kenyatta, whose birth name was Donald Jackson, had done well since leaving Mississippi. He had attended Harvard Divinity School, where he was a Merrill Fellow in 1973-1974, and he subsequently earned a law degree from Harvard Law School. However, evidence showed that his activities in Mississippi and in other states were not as uplifting. At one point, after leaving the state, he joined a group that demanded $500 million in reparations from white churches and synagogues. A police officer from Pennsylvania testified that he had intimidated him and others at a church function where Kenyatta had made his demands.

Other evidence revealed that he had been the editor of a newsletter that provided instruction for making fire bombs. Further evidence showed that Kenyatta, a former minister, had violently attacked a white civil rights worker and threatened to kill him with a gun. Also it was brought out that Kenyatta was involved in a shooting incident, theft of property, and extremist activities on campuses near Jackson, Mississippi.

During the trial, the courtroom was packed with supporters of various civil rights groups and the ACLU. They packed the courtroom to attempt to influence the jurors, but it did not work. After a six-day trial, a federal jury, composed of males and females, blacks and whites, found us innocent of violating the civil rights of Kenyatta.

The ACLU had spent ten years off and on obtaining depositions from Moore, Fitzpatrick and me. I was in Washington during some of these depositions as an agent and of course they were after me because I had risen up through the ranks to deputy assistant director. During the depositions, the ACLU attorneys were rude and the language coming from their lips was unbelievable. You could just feel the hatred for the FBI.

At no time during the depositions at their offices were we ever offered refreshments. We had to ask for breaks. They were not even interested in telling us where the nearest restroom was located. In fact, they had fun at our expense in their hate-filled questions. I must say they were never kind to us. They went out of their way to ensure that we were not comfortable and could possibly lose our homes and what little we had in the bank and make it impossible for other agents to ever following instructions from the FBI.

Daiger, who was such a calm reserved individual, became so upset of the treatment toward us that it drove him harder to defend us. The Justice Department also selected Mary Mitchell, the niece of former U.S. Senator George Mitchell, as one of those individuals to assist us in the trial. Dagger, Mary Mitchell, and their staff came to Jackson, after I had retired from the FBI, several times to prepare us for the trial.

Muhammed Kenyatta died in 1992 at the age of forty-seven. Roy Moore is now deceased, as is Tom Fitzpatrick, who passed away in 2011. Tom and I communicated often through the years. Tom, a Georgetown graduate, played basketball there and was a captain in the U.S. Army. He was, in my opinion, the finest agent I had ever worked with. His work ethic was so far above other agents, along with the fact that he was intelligent. He was an outstanding witness on the stand during our six day trial.

*   *   *

Following the trial I took stock of my life and decided to begin anew. It meant leaving a great family at Deposit Guaranty Bank, but it was time to move on. In 1991, Mississippi elected a new governor, Republican Kirk Fordice, who took office in January 1992. He was a graduate of Purdue University and attended school in Memphis, along with his eventual wife, Pat. His father operated the Fordice Construction Company in Vicksburg and he worked as an engineer prior to running for governor. He was a rough, tough individual. He said you had to be tough if you are going to be in the construction business and deal with seedy people.

Starting at an early age, he watched his father being asked for kickbacks to get construction jobs and he swore he would never do that. As I recall, the first time the governor and I met, he offered me the position of Commissioner of Public Safety. I told him that during my long period with the FBI I did not have to get involved in politics to the extent that I was told who to hire and who to fire. That's one thing about the FBI. If you are an ethical person, the director of the FBI allowed you to run your division and that included New York and Chicago, where I was based as the agent in charge. Fordice told me he did not want outside political influence from legislators and I would not get any from him. He was true to his word. I did hire and fire people without telling him in advance. I only told him afterward in the event he was asked about it. I did keep his chief of staff, Andy Taggert, informed of my personnel changes.

The governor made it clear to me that if I had a sensitive situation I could go straight to him and that is something that I did on occasion. It was interesting that he was such an unusual individual. You either liked him or disliked him. There were many people who could not stand him because he told it the way he believed it.

We began 1992 with several threats against the governor's life. The threats began as soon as he took office. One came from a white male, whom the person who took the call described as someone probably in his fifties. He called to say that Fordice could "kiss his ass goodbye."

Another time, the governor's mansion received a phone call from a white female stating the governor had better start sleeping with one eye open from now on because he was going to "get it." None of the callers stayed on the line long enough for the calls to be traced.

The governor's office on the 20th floor of the Sellers Building was not immune either. On another occasion a young white male in his late twenties came to the governor's office and asked a staff person if he could speak to the governor. He was told the governor was out of the office at the time. The young man became very agitated and angry. He insisted on seeing the governor, stating that he knew that the governor was in his office.

"I know you are going to call security but I don't give a damn," he said. "I am going to see the governor because I have something for him."

We interviewed this young man and tried to satisfy his needs and answer his questions and that seemed to be enough as we never had any difficulties with him again. When I told the governor about the threats he seemed unconcerned. However, he did carry a weapon. When he walked with state troopers assigned to the Mansion, he always had his weapon on his side. One day I asked him if he was prepared to use his weapon and he said yes, and I certainly believed him because he took pride in the fact that he was a hunter and certainly he enjoyed telling us about his hunting prowess on his safari trips abroad.

On several occasions I traveled with the governor on official business, such as the time that a tornado struck a small community in Zero, Mississippi, in March 1992. I was thoroughly impressed with how the governor could raise the spirits of people in a farming community that had just lost everything of value.

During Hurricane Andrew in August 1992, we assembled all the state troopers and state employees, and we did everything we could to assist the citizens of Mississippi during the hurricane. Andrew had just devastated Florida and was headed toward the Gulf Coast. We set up camp at Camp Shelby, a U.S. army training facility in the southern part of Mississippi. As I recall, twenty-seven people died from Andrew, from Florida to Louisiana. But I saw the governor first-hand at work and doing what he did best in helping the people of Mississippi.

During 1992, the governor's first year, there was a lot going on, both across the state and in the governor's mansion. I had no idea that the governor, when I became part of his team, was not a happy camper as far as his marital situation was concerned. He sincerely believed that he was in love with his childhood sweetheart, Ann Craven, from Memphis.

I was alerted by a trooper at the Mansion that all was not well between the governor and the first lady. My instructions were that whatever you observed or heard, you kept your mouth shut and you did your job. The state troopers in the security detail respected the governor and the first lady, so it was very difficult for some of them. But they continued doing their job under difficult circumstances.

Late in 1992 the governor called me to the Mansion one Friday evening. He proceeded to tell me he and the first lady were having difficulties and he wanted me to be aware of the situation in the event he received threats against his life. During his eight years as

189

governor, Kirk Fordice was able to get new industry in Mississippi and he was considered to be an excellent governor, but when information was revealed by the news media that he had an ongoing love affair with his former high school sweetheart from Memphis, many people who had supported him began to fall to the wayside. Once, when the governor was returning from one of his visits to Memphis, he fell asleep while driving on the interstate, ran off the road, and seriously injured himself. He spent several days recuperating.

The divorce between Kirk and Pat Fordice was a bitter one, splitting the family. He later married Ann Craven and that marriage also ended in divorce. During this time I became very close to the governor because he needed someone to talk to. I was with him when he went to sign divorce papers.

During June 1996 there was a rash of black church burnings across the South. We had some in Mississippi, which we resolved by aggressive investigation. President Bill Clinton called a conference in Washington for states that were having the church burnings. He invited governors, attorneys general, and anyone else the governors wanted to bring. Fordice did not care for Clinton and Clinton did not care for him, according to Fordice. They had known each other as governors. Fordice told me I would attend the conference on his behalf.

At that time Mike Moore was the Mississippi Attorney General. Mike and I had an excellent relationship. The Attorney General was involved in the tobacco industry litigation and was not able to attend the conference. I flew to Washington on the state plane and attended, representing the governor and the State of Mississippi. There were governors and attorneys general, plus vice president Al Gore and the president. When it came time for me to present what we had accomplished in Mississippi, I handled that and sat down.

As the conference ended, I headed to the door to go to the airport and heard this voice saying, "Jim, Jim." I turned around and a secret service agent said the president wanted to see me.

The president walked over and put his arm around my waist.

"Jim, that was an excellent report that you gave on the church burnings."

I said, "Thank you, Mr. President, I am most appreciative of your comments."

I did not say to the president, "Governor Fordice sends his best," nor did he tell me, "Send my best to Kirk Fordice."

The meeting at the White House was in June 1996. After I returned to Mississippi, I immediately went to the governor's mansion for a prearranged briefing for the governor on what was accomplished at the meeting. He had told me in advance that he wanted to know what each governor had reported, who they brought with them, what attorneys general were there. Then he said, "Well, when you come back let's have dinner together at the mansion," which we did.

As I told him stories of what each governor said—I could do that because I took copious notes—he sometimes laughed, but then when I told him what had occurred at the end of the meeting with President Clinton being so kind to me, he said, "Commish, you didn't fall for that crap, did you?"

"Governor, the president was very sincere," I said. "By the way, I did not give him your best regards."

"You better not have."

That was the kind of person Fordice was. He was an interesting person to be around. He was sad that he and the first lady ended up going through a contentious divorce because it made it difficult for everyone working around them. There were so many people who truly loved Pat Fordice.

But they did have a rocky marriage. Once, when the First Lady started throwing her china upstairs in the living quarters, breaking china all over the place—and it was her china by the way—the governor could not control her and he called one of the troopers to come up, hoping she would calm down.

Not knowing exactly what to do, the trooper began picking up the broken china, putting it in a waste basket. When the governor saw that, he barked, "Stop—that's not your job. That's her damn china. She broke it and she can pick it up."

Of course, the family could not blame their mother because the governor was slipping off to Memphis to see another woman. I was shocked to learn that the governor was going to Memphis without security. Since the governor was so negative on Bill Clinton and his affairs, I truly did not think the governor would ever follow along the same lines, so to speak. But he did.

The divorce was anything but amicable. The governor hurt himself severely among his friends and followers with his split from the First Lady. She was very popular and became even more popular after their divorce. She had her own radio program. She did commercials. She was very a high profile person across the state. In my opinion, her celebrity was richly deserved.

Later, the governor married the other woman, Ann Craven from Memphis—and their marriage also was rocky. My wife, Marie, and I were together with them on occasion. The governor did not approve of her drinking in public and they had words over this in my presence.

When he and Pat divorced, the governor asked that I go with him when he signed his divorce papers. The same thing happened when he and Ann Craven divorced. He again asked me to accompany him to sign the papers. Apparently, I was the go-to guy for divorce paper signing.

*   *   *

Governor Fordice knew how to assemble people and how to let those individuals do their job. I was extremely impressed with his cabinet. This group worked well together and there was no rancor in the meetings, no attempt to impress the governor because he was not one you worked to impress. During the time I was with the governor, he had several chiefs of staff, including Andy Taggert and Mark Henry. I had good relationships with both Andy and Mark. There was no rancor or distrust when I went straight to the governor to report to him on issues about which he had asked to be kept informed.

Early one Sunday he called me to the Mansion. He had received information regarding an individual who told staff that he was going to expose the governor. I conducted the investigation myself. As it turned out, the individual was just a teenage kid. The governor was concerned because the teen told me about the governor's trips to Memphis. I didn't know until later that the governor was making those trips, even before he became governor. I found out that this young kid was playing games and he really knew nothing about any trips the governor had taken. The individual was told to stop calling to say he was going to expose the governor. Shortly after that he moved from Mississippi.

Several movies were made in Mississippi during the time that the governor was in office. *Ghosts of Mississippi* was one of them. As I recall, the governor refused to allow the mansion to be used in filming some of the segments on Byron de la Beckwith. We also had the filming of the *Chamber*. It was filmed in October 1996. Gene Hackman was the star and again we tried to work with those individuals, not so much the governor as the highway patrol. In the movie *A Time to Kill*, John Grisham's bestseller, I went out of my way to assist the producers of this movie. They wanted advice about the uniforms, the cars, everything related to law enforcement, because the highway patrol was depicted in this movie filmed in Canton. I spent quite some time at the location and was asked my opinion on a number of issues.

A Time to Kill was a film that received nationwide attention since it was based on Grisham's book and filmed on location in Mississippi. Joel Schumacher was the director and producer and he was fair to all of us, extremely kind. And Matthew McConaughey, Samuel Jackson and Sandra Bullock were outstanding in the film. Keifer Sutherland was a Klansman in the movie and I watched him in the different scenes and he was just absolutely tremendous. I think this film was good for Mississippi. Certainly it was a far cry from *Mississippi Burning*. I always said that film was a collection of fact and fiction concocted by Hollywood.

In January 1993, I was asked to appear on the Larry King Live show in Washington to talk about the Klan and the book written by Jack Nelson, *Attack on Terror.* I mentioned this to the governor. He scoffed but he did not say, "Ingram, I do not want you to go." So I went.

I had advised Andy Taggert, chief of staff, I was going. It was a very exciting time and I invited Larry King to visit Mississippi. He said there were only two states he had not visited and one was Mississippi. But King treated me extremely well.

Not too long after that, I was asked by Terrell Bolton if I would come to Dallas and speak on his behalf as he was being appointed the first black chief of the Dallas Police Department. I consented and told the governor that I was going to travel to Dallas and speak on Bolton's behalf. In fact, the mayor at that time in Dallas was Ron Kirk, who appointed Bolton. I was very impressed with

Mayor Kirk. Later he was asked to join President Obama's cabinet as U.S. Trade Representative.

* * *

The governor liked to refer to Attorney General Mike Moore, a Democrat, as Flashbulb Mike. He certainly did not care for the way Mike Moore handled his duties as attorney general. Even after he left office, the governor and I had many spirited discussions about Mike Moore. I told the governor, straight on, that I was a friend of Mike Moore and he had always treated me and law enforcement straight. Mike and I started the law enforcement appreciation breakfast, with the help of business people, for metro police officers. Mike and I always had an excellent and friendly relationship. I felt no hesitation in letting the governor know that.

There were several times, as we headed out to dinner, that we discussed Mike Moore. By the tone of his voice I could almost hear him thinking, "All right, Commish, take me back home." Invariably, my wife, Marie, sensing the governor's rising emotional temperature, would interject and say, "Let's not talk politics right now." And so it would pass.

We often attended the Thursday night buffet at the restaurant in the Wathall, a downtown hotel that had a long, colorful history. The governor always reveled in the attention he received from the staff and other diners. One of the people he sometimes encountered there was a lady from Rankin County, Debby Gambling, who wrote letters to the editor all the time to express her conservative views. She and the governor had a friendly relationship over the governor's dog, Lance. On many occasions Debby would take Lance while the governor was away and he was always appreciative of that. I remember that he thought highly of her.

After retirement, we got together and rambled about the back roads of Mississippi, selecting places to eat. I always drove because after one or two times with him driving, I realized he never paid attention to the road. He was always talking and looking around every which way but the road. He considered himself an excellent pilot, but I would never fly with him. He had his personal plane at a hanger in Madison, not too far from where we both lived. And he would get upset with me when I refused to go up with him on a solo flight.

I said, "Governor, I made a vow to never go up in a plane with only one pilot." That wasn't entirely true. I had heard stories of when he took control of the state plane now and then and the pilots would allow him to set the plane down and they had some pretty tough landings. Richard, the state pilot, had to remind him once in a while how to pull up and let down and they had some rough landings.

The governor loved his dog, Lance. He took great pride in that dog and felt that he could do anything that he wanted to do. He took the dog up in the plane and he would go to lunches and dinners with that dog. I would sometimes say, "Governor, there is really not enough room in my pickup truck for Lance." That would upset him now and then, but he knew what I was talking about. A radio program once carried a statement by me about the governor's dog, who was his constant companion, and a friend relayed it to the governor. He was once told by a host at a dinner, "You may want to take your dog to the backyard where he can use the facilities."

The governor responded, "Look, that dog pees when I tell him to pee. He does not have to go outside to use your facilities."

I laughed at that. Andy Taggert used that in one of his books, *Mississippi Politics*. The governor allowed that dog to do whatever it wanted. He thought it was humorous when Lance chased the women around the Mansion. They did not fear Lance, but they did not like it when he jumped up in their laps. The governor would just laugh and not call off the dog. I told the governor, "I don't think that's funny."

"Well, I do."

That was just the way he felt.

I was also familiar with the governor's riding habits. He thought he was quite a horseman, but like with a car or a plane he had his difficult times on a horse. He was thrown many times. People laughed, but it was not funny. One thing about Kirk Fordice, he was one tough son of a gun, and I enjoyed being around him.

* * *

We had some tough days in the Mississippi Highway Patrol. In any law enforcement agency, you have suicides of employees, no matter what you do. Sometimes what you do is never enough. Every organization has employees for whom the stress becomes more than some individuals can handle. That certainly happened in the Highway Patrol. When those things occurred it was always a very sad thing to deal with.

I was fortunate in managing the Highway Patrol in that I had some leaders who followed my philosophy and management style. I had Tom Ward as my chief of the patrol, and Marvin Curtis as assistant chief of the patrol. In addition, we had some outstanding captains in the districts who helped us function properly.

Gov. Fordice's marital problems made him fodder for the news media. That prompted him to circle the wagons, so to speak. He had only a few people around him that he trusted. One of them was Captain Jody Rigby of the Highway Patrol.

After the governor's accident on his way home from Memphis, he was the butt of many jokes around the state, but it never deterred him from leading the state forward. One of his closest friends was Pat Taylor, a wealthy oil magnate from New Orleans. He and the governor went on African safaris together, spending weeks hunting on the African trails.

Taylor had a 4,000-acre ranch in south Mississippi, Circle Bar Ranch, and once a year he would host an all-day celebration for law enforcement for Mississippi, Louisiana, and any other state that wanted to participate. Law enforcement officers from all over traveled to the Circle Bar Ranch, which had its own airport, to enjoy catfish lunch, soft drinks, fellowship, pistol matches, games and a tour of the grounds. He had every type of animal imaginable roaming the ranch, including several African species.

Pat Taylor and the governor were very close, but Pat was a politician and he always had the governor from Louisiana as well as the governor from Mississippi. He always had me say a few words to the assembled group and I always enjoyed that. After the governor was injured he missed the festivities one year and I was asked by Pat Taylor to say a few words on behalf of the governor, which I did.

Then Louisiana Governor Edwards got up to speak. Of course, he and Fordice were not close by any means. But Edwards knew how to handle a crowd, and Pat Taylor had a large auditorium, so he wasn't about to allow it to go to waste.

"You know, Kirk Fordice and I are entirely two different people," Edwards said. "He has women problems and I have never

196

had women problems. Women love me, no matter what age, but the governor seems to have a difficult time with women."

Everyone had a huge laugh.

Edwards followed up with, "My only problem is that the federal people will not leave me alone."

As we all know, Edwards was later convicted in federal court and sent to prison.

When I returned to Jackson, the governor asked me what happened that day. I told him of Edwards' remarks. He did not find that amusing because he felt everyone was taking advantage of him. But I had to give it to Edwards. He knew how to command attention.

*   *   *

In January 2000, the governor left office.

Early in 2004 the governor became very ill. Since he had purchased a home in Madison and I lived in Madison, I would take him food and try to attend to his needs. Previously, during the years he was in office, we would get together and go to dinner, lunch or breakfast, sometimes traveling the back roads of Mississippi. Typically, we argued back and forth, usually about politics. Whenever needed, two troopers, Jody Rigby and Tyrone Lockhart, picked up the governor and took him to the University Medical Center for treatment. The governor knew he was dying and he attempted to give me some of his mementos, which I refused.

I said, "No governor, you're all right."

He wanted me to take a memento of the USS Stennis, the aircraft carrier, which was sent to him by the admiral. I had accompanied him to Virginia when we toured the aircraft carrier and when they sent him this ship he said, "I want you to have it."

I told him he would recover.

During the summer, I called the First Lady to tell her that the governor was in very poor health and needed family attention. She said, "Let Craven handle it."

"She's gone," I said. "They're in the process of divorce and it's about to come through. She will not be returning. The governor told her never to return, at least that's what he told me."

I told the First Lady that the governor needed her, the sons and the daughter, Angie, who I had always admired for her feistiness

197

because she took after her father. Angie responded and came to Madison to take care of her father.

When the governor's health took a turn for the worse, I called Pat Taylor in New Orleans and told Pat, "I'm with the governor each day"—and the governor and I were out of government at that time. I said, "Pat, the governor is in serious condition and if you intend to see him alive you need to come to Jackson.

"I'll get my plane—I'm on my way," he said. "Can you have people meet me?"

I said I would.

We met at Kirk's house and Pat was shocked at the appearance of the governor. Not long after that visit the governor passed away at the hospital on September 7, 2004, surrounded by his family.

At the First Lady's request, I accompanied her and her son, Dan, to Wright and Ferguson Funeral Home. Pat asked me if the governor had a burial policy.

I said, "No."

"How do you know?"

"Because I attempted to take him through the funeral grounds to show him my plot in a mausoleum."

He said, "I'm not interested where you are going to be buried and I'm not interested in a plot right now."

Many times, when I tried to turn in off the Highland Colony Parkway, he would say, "I know what you are trying to do so keep driving."

Pat, her son Dan, Tom and myself sat down in Tom's office and they worked out the purchase of two plots—one for the governor, and next to the governor, one for the First Lady.

While we were sitting there, Pat made a call on her cell phone to country music star Marty Stuart, originally from Philadelphia, Mississippi. In my presence she told him about the death of the governor and asked Marty if he could attend the services and if he would play his mandolin, sing or whatever he wanted to do.

Marty told Pat he had just arrived in Nashville. He said he would check his schedule, because he knew he would have to cancel some dates, but he would be in Jackson for the funeral. Marty did come to Jackson and he played his mandolin beautifully at the services.

Immediately upon the death of former Governor Kirk Fordice, sitting Governor Haley Barbour appointed his chief of staff Charlie Williams, Danny Cooper, a businessman, and myself to meet and coordinate plans for the funeral of the governor. I was honored that the governor included me in this group. The governor and First Lady Marsha were so gracious because they had a long friendship with Kirk and Pat.

Three years later, on July 2, 2007, Pat passed away of cancer. She was a remarkable person. Again, I was honored that Governor Barbour asked that I coordinate with the family the funeral of First Lady Pat Fordice. They were buried together at the Wright and Ferguson Cemetery on Highland Colony Parkway, just outside of Jackson.

Jim Ingram in his home office with cold case file in 2008
© Photo by James L. Dickerson

14

RETURN OF THE WITNESS HUNTER

In 2004 I was retired, but I was always getting calls from people asking for my help in criminal or legal matters. One of the calls I received was from Charlie Saums, the founder of Security Support Services, one of the largest investigative agencies in the South. He handled high profile clients across the country. A former police officer himself, he is one of the finest investigators in the country and his work speaks for itself.

One of the things I like about Charlie is that he is a tough, no-nonsense guy who can handle himself in any situation. If you put him in a pen with a bunch of pit bull dogs, the pit bulls would be yelping to get out because Charlie would whip every one of them.

Charlie asked me if I would review some data involving a murder charge against an individual up in Kentucky. The young man, Lucas Goodrum, was charged with raping and killing Melissa Katie Autry, a freshman student at Western Kentucky University. The case was about to come to trial and the headlines in some of the print media were that he was a rich kid whose stepfather was related to the founder of Dollar General and his family was shelling out huge sums of money for the best defense possible.

I was asked to review some tapes of the interviews with Goodrum and others and furnish my comments. I enjoyed working on this matter for Charlie and traveling to Kentucky to testify at the trial. Goodrum was acquitted by a jury on all charges.

* * *

In late 2004, Bob Garrity, who was then agent in charge of the Jackson FBI office, approached me about assisting the FBI in the Neshoba County retrial of Edgar Ray Killen, then eighty years of age. Killen had been among the defendants in the 1967 federal court trial in which eighteen defendants were charged with conspiracy to deprive the three civil rights workers killed near Philadelphia of their civil rights. Jurors were unable to reach a verdict on three of the defendants, including Killen, the Baptist preacher who was accused of masterminding the plot.

Garrity asked if I would assist Attorney General Jim Hood and Mark Duncan, the local district attorney in Philadelphia. The FBI needed someone who knew what had occurred in the 1960s. Since I had supervised the trial against the Klansmen for the killing of Goodman, Chaney and Schwerner, he thought I would be perfect to work with them. After giving this matter considerable thought, I knew I wanted to help the FBI. It was an opportunity to get back into the thick of things and help some people.

I was a little surprised at the extensive vetting procedure I had to go through to work for the FBI again. I underwent a background check, just as I did when I first applied for a position with the FBI, along with a credit history check, and I had to provide proof of birth. Once completed I was given an "Interim Secret" security clearance and provided with restricted access to FBI facilities to review files, identify witnesses, and conduct any other "logical" activities related to the investigations assigned to me.

After an absence of 24 years it was nice to be back in the FBI fold once again. I knew some of the original informants that were still around in Mississippi. I knew that the FBI agents who had testified in other trials had moved out of the state. They would be perfect to bring back to assist the state. The backbone of the FBI has been domestic intelligence, gathering information from informants. FBI agents in Mississippi and other Southern states were outstanding in infiltrating the Klan. We were able to defeat the Klan because we placed our informants in positions to give us the information we needed.

Converting an individual into an informant is not a simple task. You have to nurture an individual and lead him to his own conclusion that he wants to help. Yes, we paid informants, but in some situations we had informants who refused to take pay. I was very good at developing black informants also. I had the best black informant in Mississippi in the 1960s. He was astounding as he knew everything that was going on in the black communities.

One of our secret weapons in the 1960s was the wives of Klansmen. Because they were usually more practical than their husbands—and had a lot at stake in their husband's illegal ventures—we appealed to their practical side and to their wish to protect their family.

Agents would watch a known Klansman's home and when the Klansman left for work or to attend a Klan rally, the agents approached the home if they thought the wife was there alone. They'd knock on the door and when it opened they would identify themselves and ask the wife if her husband was at home.

When the wife said no, they'd respond with the line, "Well, would you mind too much if we come in for a cup of coffee?"

Typically, the wife would invite them inside and pour them a cup of coffee. Southern hospitality existed even in Klan homes.

After a decent amount of coffee sipping and small talk, one of the agents, using a stern voice, would let the wife know the FBI knew all about her husband's involvement with the Klan. Shaking his head the agent would comment that it was too bad that he probably was headed to prison because of his activities with the Klan. The wife usually reacted as you would imagine, with shock and surprise.

Once they'd set the hook, the agent with the less stern voice would say something to the effect of, "That's too bad, too—him with a family and all. We'd sure hate to see that happen."

Once they had outlined the problem, one of the agents offered a solution.

"You know, we can pay your husband for his help. More than he's making in his current job."

"Really?"

"Sure."

"But what if they killed him?"

"We won't let that happen."

Sometimes the officers would leave knowing the wife would confront her husband, not only with "What has the Klan ever done for you?"—but with practical questions such as, "If they are going to be giving out money, why shouldn't we get our share? The children need new shoes for school."

You'd be truly surprised how often that tactic worked.

* * *

Once I sat down and talked to Garrity he explained what he expected from me and I agreed to his terms. He said I would be working with current FBI agent Billy Stokes, a native Mississippian from south Mississippi. Billy had been assigned the task of investigating Mississippi's cold-case civil rights violations and he was given the authority to hire me as an independent contractor. Billy offered me $60 an hour to work with him.

I told him he didn't have to pay me anything. It'd be an honor to work the cases.

"But it's illegal if you do this voluntarily," he explained. "I have to sign you on and get you a secret clearance."

Billy, I discovered, was one of the finest FBI agents the Bureau has ever had. He came up through the ranks after receiving his education in Mississippi. He served in several field offices, worked in the forensic lab in Washington, and testified in cases all over the world. Stokes told me we would be a tandem.

"We'll be the Lone Ranger and Tonto," he explained. "You'd be the Lone Ranger."

"Oh, my!" I responded. *Who wouldn't want to be the Lone Ranger?*

* * *

On our first trip together, we were cruising on Interstate 20 to Meridian, when I asked him how fast he was driving.

"Seventy-one, sir," Billy said.

"I don't have all day—let's go."

"But I don't want to get pulled over and ticketed."

"You kidding me?" I asked. "I hired every highway patrolman on this road."

Billy bumped it up to 95 and off we went.

"Rule of thumb," I said. "You ride with me, don't worry about the speed limit."

One day we realized we needed to talk to a retired FBI agent who once had arrested a KKK member involved in one of our cases. He had since moved to Miami.

"We need to head down to Miami to talk to him," said Billy.

"You know I don't like to fly commercial."

"Well, Jim, I can work around that."

"How you going to do that?"

"Don't worry about it."

Billy called some FBI pilots that he was on good terms with asked if they could bring an aircraft to Jackson so that he could take me to Miami. They told him the FBI director was not using his plane that week. Would he be interested in that plane?

The answer, of course, was a resounding yes.

204

The director's plane was a Citation with Rolls-Royce engines. It was the fastest private plane made at that time, with a luxurious interior. Of course, I was aware of none of that.

When we arrived at the airport, I was convinced we would be leaving in propeller driven plane. It so happened that U.S. Senator Thad Cochran and other dignitaries also were at the airport waiting for a plane.

"That big Citation rolled up," recalls Billy, "and I said, 'Jim your ride is here—let's go.'"

Everyone, including me, looked at the Citation and someone asked "Who's he riding with?"

"I can't tell you," responded Billy.

Billy had asked the pilots to wear their fight uniforms and they did. Once the plane stopped, they rolled out a red carpet with great flourish. Dressed like they were leading a Fourth of July parade, they went inside the airport and said, "Mr. Ingram, your ride is here."

Explains Billy: "It was a sanctioned flight, all above board. Jim was in poor health and I didn't want him to ride commercial."

* * *

Billy wanted to make sure I used my experience with former Klan members and other associates during the old days, so that between the two of us we could identify potential witnesses. We scoured the state and we traveled out of state to locate former Klansman and witnesses who still might have information about the case. Doors were slammed in our face. Others greeted us warmly. I was shocked at how many people still remembered me after so many years.

Soon they began calling me the witness hunter, and I relished that title. After sitting down with Jim Hood, Mark Duncan, assistant attorney general Lee Martin, and Jim Gilliland, who was the state attorney general's office investigator, I understood what they expected. I knew all the old players. I knew they had, up until 2001, an excellent witness in Cecil Price, the deputy sheriff from Neshoba County who was convicted in 1967. Price accidentally fell off a cherry picker while working and died two or three days later. I knew another witness, Bob Stringer, having met Stringer in south Mississippi during Sam Bowers' trial. As a young man, Stringer worked for Sam Bowers and hung around Bowers at his

Laurel, Mississippi home and traveled with him. Whenever Bowers met with people, Stringer overheard the conversations. But there was too much pressure on Bob Stringer and he committed suicide in March 2004.

I knew James McIntyre extremely well. Still do at the time of this writing. McIntyre, who was Killen's attorney, was also Rainey's attorney back in the 1960s. When James gave his memoirs to the civil rights museum he called me and wanted me to come to his office and review the data with him before he turned it over to the museum. It was a collection of letters, threats against Rainey, threats against others, and it is interesting reading.

I had known Judge Marcus Gordon, who was an outstanding judge in Mississippi, and one who had the temperament to handle the Killen trial. I knew the array of potential suspects, so it was interesting that I had a chance to come back to start reviewing the old files, informant files and others with Agent Stokes.

The first thing Marc Duncan, Jim Hood, and Lee Martin wanted was the complete federal trial transcript that had taken place in September 1967. The file was voluminous. By the time it was copied it filled a truck. I personally hand-carried those copies to Marc Duncan and his investigator Larry Walker, who had worked for the Mississippi Highway Patrol while I was the commissioner. I knew Larry as a very competent investigator and an honest individual in every way who lived outside Philadelphia.

Dick Molpus, former secretary of state, was from Philadelphia, and he had spoken out at the right time and it had a healing effect for Mississippi and I give him great credit for this, along with comments from Mississippi Governor Haley Barbour.

As Stokes and I traveled to interview potential witnesses, we went to one city to contact an old informant that we thought could assist us. He certainly wanted nothing to do with us, but he was kind enough to allow us into his dining room, where the entire table top was filled with bottles of prescription medicine. I had never witnessed so many drugs in my life. After spending a few minutes with him, we knew he could never be a witness.

We had individuals who asked us to leave their property. We did. But we kept going back until we agreed that we had gotten everything we needed from that individual, still being kind enough to that person that you never shut the door behind you. We went down false trails, where people would tell us new things that in most cases never panned out.

Earlier in the book, I set out in detail the trial in September 1967 and critiqued the FBI's handling of the investigation. One of the things I pointed out this go around was that Baptist minister Killen was not convicted in 1967 because one lone female juror from south Mississippi stated she just could not believe that a minister would be involved in killing anyone. To convict him this time, prosecutors would have to address that mindset.

Once the relationship between the state attorney general's office and the FBI was locked into place, the prosecution of Edgar Ray Killen began in earnest. It began with interviews with Klansman Billy Wayne Posey, who had implicated Killen in the Philadelphia murders after receiving a guarantee from prosecutors that they would not use his statements against him. The next step was to take Posey before the Neshoba County grand jury to testify about his knowledge of the murders of Schwerner, Goodman, and Chaney. Leaving the grand jury room, the 69-year-old Posey was surrounded by reporters. He told them he thought it was ridiculous for the murders to be revisited all these years later.

Posey's testimony was instrumental in the grand jury returning an indictment on Killen, charging him with felony manslaughter. On January 7, 2005, Killen pleaded not guilty to three counts of manslaughter, thus becoming the focus of the first state charges in the forty-year-old murders. Six days later he reported to the Neshoba County Courthouse in Philadelphia to stand trial. Waiting for him was a gathering of Klansmen who had come to the courthouse to demonstrate their support of him.

When sufficient evidence was gathered to retry Killen, it was still very difficult because we had people on the stand reading excerpts from the trial in 1967. That was difficult for the jurors to trace back what had occurred forty years before. But we had live witnesses from the FBI, most notably Jay Cochran, with whom I spent hours, and he is a dear friend today. One of the telling parts of the trial was the testimony of Mike Hatcher. Mike had been an FBI informant when he was a young Meridian police officer and it was difficult for Mike to testify in 1967. It was even more difficult for him to testify in 2005. Defense attorneys attempted to show that there was a difference between his 1967 transcript and his testimony in at the 2005 trial.

The average person could not imagine the pressure that was on Hatcher because he knew that whatever he did in 1967 was going to harm him, even though he was a police officer. There were death threats, threats to his family, difficulty maintaining a job, and he experienced all of that. But Mike ended up making an outstanding witness because of what Killen had imparted to him. It was not previously brought out, but I have talked with Mike about this. Mike Hatcher was one of the police officers involved in the shootout with Thomas Tarrants when Tarrants attempted to kill Myer Davidson, a Jewish business person in Meridian in the 1960s. Tarrants ended up shooting Hatcher three times, as I recall. It looked for a while that Hatcher would not survive, but he did. So Hatcher has paid his dues.

Mike told me that every now and then he and Tarrants had conversed over the years, talking about the shoot out. It is interesting to note that after Mike recovered, he went to the hospital to confront Tarrants, to tell him, "I'm officer Mike Hatcher, the police officer you shot three times with your machine gun." He just wanted to let Tarrants know he was a better man than he was and a survivor. It took guts for Mike Hatcher to do all that and even more to come back and testify again. He could have easily said no and walked away because he knew he would still have to put up with some people who felt he was wrong in 1967 and wrong again in 2005.

I always admired that he was a standup guy. He took on all comers, and he was fearless. Hatcher told me that after his testimony against Killen in June 2005, he had to resign from his employment because of harassment by some of the employees. He had threats against his life, proving that old hatreds never die. Many of the Klan members and sympathizers never forgave him for being a standup guy for law enforcement.

The circus atmosphere that existed at Killen's 1967 trial was the same as at the 2005 trial, with reporters and television cameras from all over the country. The atmosphere of the 1960s returned, with state and federal authorities doing exactly what they had to do to maintain order. They set up headquarters across the street from the courthouse. The FBI brought in personnel with computers that checked on suspicious individuals traveling to the trial. The sheriff was outstanding, as was the Mississippi Highway Patrol.

James McIntyre, one of Killen's attorneys, whom I had mentioned earlier, was Rainey's attorney in the 1967 trail. James defended him well because Rainey was not convicted. James and I have discussed the two trials over the years. James told me the FBI did not receive the credit it deserved, either from blacks or whites, because of public hostility to the FBI. The state wanted the 2005 trail to be a state controlled trial, but as James said, without the transcript he does not believe Killen would have been convicted. I go back again to the story about Mike Hatcher, the way he was treated during both trials.

Informants have always been attacked when they appeared in court and grilled about their relationship with the FBI, especially on the issue of whether they were paid and, if so, how much? Delmar Dennis, who testified in 1967 for the FBI, was attacked because he had been close to Bowers and was perceived to be a traitor to the Klan's beliefs.

Wallace Miller, the Meridian police officer, who testified in 1967, was a member of the Klan and an FBI informant. He was given a hard time. Bill Ray Pitts, a cooperating witness for the FBI who was the key witness in the conviction of Sam Bowers in 1998—all paid a price in their various communities for being a good citizen and doing the right thing.

*   *   *

The one thing I will always remember out of the trial was that six of the prosecution's fourteen witnesses were "from the grave," meaning their testimony was read from transcripts. That was essential to place the civil rights workers at the Mount Zion Methodist Church and to prove the admissions that Killen had so arrogantly and recklessly made to individuals outside the courtroom.

For example, the day after the murders, Killen went to Klansman Joseph M. Hatcher to give him a gun. At that time, it was established in court that he did not hesitate to admit his involvement in the crime to Hatcher. On another occasion, Killen attended the Pine Grove Baptist Church and had a conversation with a man in the presence of his 10-year-old grandson who later, as an adult, vividly remembered the conversation in which Killen admitted his part in the killings and said he was proud of it. Some memories never die.

Some of the most poignant testimony came from Michael Schwerner's wife, Rita Schwerner, who conveyed the pain she suffered over losing her husband. She was with her husband in Mississippi and recounted the telephone threats she received on a regular basis. They had to move often, moving from house to house, because the only accommodations they could find were with black families and once their location was known they had to move so that the black family they lived with would not be threatened. The prosecution's case ended with the emotional testimony of Fannie Lee Chaney, the eighty-two year-old mother of the murdered James Chaney. By the time she finished, there was nothing else to say. The prosecution rested.

Easily the most dramatic moments in the trail came from Jim Hood, who began his closing argument with the words, "Evil flourishes when good people sit idly by and do nothing," and then proceeded to show the jury a photograph of Killen as a young man, radiating innocence. He wondered aloud the mystery of how such innocence could transform into evil.

At one point, Hood walked over to Killen and pointed directly at him, saying "There evil sits. It's seething behind those glasses."

"Shut up, you son of a bitch!" Killen blurted out, losing control.

Killen's true character shined through brightly. It was enough to earn him a conviction and a 60-year prison sentence for manslaughter.

* * *

To the surprise of many, Killen, who attended his trial in a wheelchair and maintained that he was unable to walk, was set free on $600,000 bond while his appeal was filed by his attorneys. After local newspapers reported that Killen had misrepresented his physical condition in court and had been spotted moving around the county without the use of a wheelchair—and word circulated of a "Killen Appreciation Day" that had been organized by white supremacists—Judge Gordon ordered Killen back to jail.

The Mississippi Supreme Court ruled against the bizarre arguments set forth by Killen's attorneys that if he had been prosecuted in the 1960s his case would have been tried before an all-white jury and he would have been found innocent because at that time it was not considered a crime for a white man to kill an African American. In other words, justice delayed was justice denied for Preacher Killen. Appalled by that argument, the state high court said it was "surprised" that it was ever made. The trial and sentence were upheld by the Supreme Court.

* * *

The FBI received international and national attention for its cooperation with state officials in the 2005 trial and certainly FBI officials were pleased with that recognition. The SAC of the Jackson office, Robert Garrity, did such a masterful job in the 2005 case that I told him, "Pack your bags, you are headed to Washington." And that was exactly what happened. Before the year was over, he was transferred to Washington, where he was named deputy chief information officer for the FBI.

* * *

The second cold case that Billy Stokes asked me to assist him with was the 1964 kidnapping and murder of Charles Moore and Henry Dee of Meadville, Mississippi. The reopening of this case took a circuitous route. For many years, the two main suspects in the case—Charles Edwards and James Ford Seale—had disappeared from public view. If anyone ever thought about them, and that didn't happen too often, it was assumed that both men had long since departed this earth.

All that came to an end in 2004 when David Ridgen, a producer with Canadian Broadcasting Corporation, decided to come to Mississippi to do a documentary on the so-called "wrong bodies" found during the search for Goodman, Chaney and Schwerner. After finding a living relative of Charles Moore—his brother, Thomas—he telephoned Donna Ladd, editor of the weekly *Jackson Free Press*, to ask if the newspaper planned coverage of the Killen trial. She told him she wasn't certain since the newspaper was in the process of investigating the long-forgotten murders of Moore and Dee. Delighted, Ridgen asked if they could work together on the project. That was fine with her.

When Ridgen arrived in Jackson he had with him Thomas Moore. Together, with Ladd and photographer Kate Medley, they went to Meadville to attempt to get an interview with Charles Edwards. He responded that he had no interest in talking to them about the case or anything else.

211

Edgar Ray Killen enters courthouse for sentencing
Photo by Kate Medley/Jackson Free Press

Undeterred they went to Natchez to follow several promising leads, only to discover that James Ford Seale, thought to be long dead, was alive and well in Roxie, Mississippi, where he lived in a Winnebago-type trailer.

When they drove past the trailer, they saw him assisting his wife in unloading the family car. They pulled over and shouted at him from a distance, asking if he was, indeed, James Ford Seale. But he ignored them and went inside the trailer.

They promptly telephoned U.S. Attorney Dunn Lampton and asked him about the status of the Moore and Dee case. He said he knew nothing about the case. It was before his time. They asked for a meeting with him, after which he called FBI headquarters and requested information about the status of the case. Once Lampton realized the case had never been resolved—and that two of the principle suspects were still alive—he reopened the investigation.

I was asked to assist the prosecution. No one had ever been prosecuted for the men's deaths. Forty-two years after the commission of the crimes, justice was still waiting for resolution in those gruesome murders. With a sense of urgency, Agent Stokes and I again teamed up and hit the road.

We traveled to the very spot where Moore and Dee had been beaten in the Homochitta Forest and then tossed, bruised and bleeding, their mouths covered by duct tape, into the trunk of a car and driven in darkness through the night to an unknown destination. Then, using Stokes' global positioning device, we traveled to the area over in Louisiana where Moore and Dee had been taken, both knowing full well what their fate would be—death. It took us two and a half hours in 2006 and 2007 to make that trip, so you can imagine what the drive would have been on the roads of that time.

When Billy and I traveled to Tallulah to track down who might still be alive at the Madison Parish Sheriff's office, we were very pleased that we were able to find three outstanding witnesses. Roland Mitchell, who was then frail and had health problems, was not sure at first he would be able to come to Jackson and handle appearing in court. Stokes and I assured all of them we would come back, pick them up, take them to Jackson, place them in a hotel one half-block from the court, stay with them, and see that their every desire was taken care of. We would then stay with them and return them to their homes in Louisiana.

They realized how important and historic this matter was that they told us what they recalled about finding the bodies. They said that the stench from the torsos was so bad they did not take the body bags into the funeral home, but instead had to put the body bags in the square in the open air, where they baked under 100 degree heat. They also told the story about placing the call to Sheriff Rainey in Philadelphia, telling Rainey they had found the bodies, meaning Goodman, Chaney and Schwerner.

That's when Rainey turned the phone over to Deputy Cecil Price, who at no time gave any hint that these bodies could not be the missing civil rights workers, because he knew they were buried in an earthen dam.

During this time, Stokes and I were still going out and looking for witnesses. One witness we wanted was J. K. Greer, a Province Grand Giant for the White Knights of the Klan in southwest Mississippi. He lived in Natchez, and he and FBI agent Billy Bob Williams had become very good friends; therefore we knew that Greer could tell us a few things about the Klan and hopefully about Seale since he knew Seale personally.

On our first encounter with Greer, he did not want to talk to us, but we told him we would be back and we did return. I can well remember on a cold day he invited us out on his porch. He had cats and you could tell where the cats had been all over the place, soiling everything, so I did not even sit down.

Stokes sat down to take notes. First thing you know one of the cats jumped on his back. Stokes jumped and hit at the cat to knock him off his back, and then the cat jumped on his shoulder. He swatted him off. I'm still standing there, laughing and Greer is amused himself. I thought any moment Stokes would lose his cool, but he never did.

A few minutes later the cat jumped on top of Stokes' head. When that happened, Stokes jumped up and roared, "I think I have all I want. I don't need any more from you, Greer."

We left and returned another day. This time he invited us inside the house. All the time I could see Billy staring down the hallway. There was no one else in the house except Stokes and Greer and myself. After we left I asked, "Why were you staring down the hallway?"

He said, "I could see a damn cat and I was waiting for that damn cat to come up the hallway after me and I was going to explode."

I got a big kick out of that. Stokes was a person that all the agents looked up to. He was the guy who could do it all. There was not anything in the bureau that he could not handle. He had worked all the big cases. I love to tell the cat story. Stokes had everything an agent needed, except cat savvy. I always wondered why the cat went after him and not me.

One of the witnesses for Seale that Billy thought he might befriend was Jack Davis. When Seale was first arrested in 1964 and transported to Jackson for questioning, Davis, who worked as a barber in Franklin County, saw Seale after his return from Jackson and heard Seale complain that he had been abused by the FBI while in custody.

Engaging Davis in conversation, Billy told him he remembered that he once had cut his hair.

"I did not cut your hair," said Davis, indignant at the suggestion. "I would not cut your hair."

In other words, Davis was saying he wanted to have nothing to do with Stokes.

Billy kept saying, "Yes . . . yes . . . you did cut my hair because you did such a bad job that my mama kept asking me who'd cut my hair."

That didn't make Davis any happier.

Much of our witness hunting centered in and around Natchez. I went into the interviews unarmed because as a contractor I was not allowed to carry a gun. Billy was the one with the gun. One day we approached a Klansman's house and Billy asked if I minded going through the door first, explaining, "If this guy sees me he isn't going to want to talk. Do you mind going first?"

"Yeah, I'll go."

Recalls Billy: "He goes up to the back door and knocks and the old guy comes to the door. Jim tells him who he is. The man is not too sure. Jim explains a little more. The guy says, 'Yeah, yeah, yeah—I remember who you are,' so he lets him into the house and I walk in behind him. There is a .38-caliber revolver on the kitchen table right where the man has been sitting and I think, oh, my word!' So I maneuver around so that I could be between the gun and him, thinking *oh this isn't good*. To make matters worse, the guy is a veteran of the Air Force from World War II and he had all these guns and stuff in the room. We sat there for an hour and a half talking to the guy and then we left. When we walked out of the house, I said, 'Jim what was the first thing you saw when you walked into the house?"

"You talking about that 38?"

Yeah. Going in that way was a bad idea."

'Why?"

'You went in unarmed."

"He wasn't going to get to that 38."

"Are you serious?"

"No Billy Boy, he wasn't going to get to that 38. I was going to get to it first."

On another trip we returned to Natchez to talk to C. G. Prosper, who was the original case agent in the Seale case. We knew he didn't want to look at an FBI agent. He didn't want to talk to one. He didn't want to see those three letters lined up together. He was a good, honest guy, so I called him up and told him I needed to come out and talk to him.

He said, "It ain't gonna happen."

"You were the case agent."

"I don't care."

Billy and I talked about it and I agreed to help him out. "I'll get you in the house. Talk about anything you want to, but don't talk about the case."

"Fair enough."

"So we go in and Jim gets me in the door," recalled Billy. "I found out Prosper had been an aerospace engineer before he joined the FBI. We talked about that for about an hour and then we left. I said," Now what are we going to do?"

"We are going to go back again and again. Sooner or later he'll talk."

On the fourth attempt he finally talked.

"So now the prosecutor wants me to get him to testify," says Billy. "I said, 'Are you kidding? I can't get the guy out of the house. How am I going to get him to the courthouse?'"

Billy drives down to Natchez to get him and he looks at him and says, "I'll go with you, but Jim has to go with me."

"Are you kidding me?" Billy says. "Jim won't want to ride all the way down here to pick you up."

"I'll ride up there with you to Jackson if Jim is at the courthouse. Then I'll go in."

Billy says, "All right."

So Billy drives down to Natchez to get him and when they arrive at the courthouse in Jackson, he asks, "Is Jim in the courtroom."

"Yes, he is in the courtroom."

I am sitting in the courtroom, waiting. When they arrive, he looks at me and says, so that I can hear him, "I'll do it, but Jim has to sit on the front row."

I moved up to the front row so that he could see me.

He testified as he had promised. When he finished, Billy drove him home. Says Billy today: "Do you think I ever would have gotten him to testify without Jim? Never would that have happened. Jim makes things happen."

*　*　*

Some forty-two years, eight months and twenty-two days after the murders of Dee and Moore, the federal government filed an indictment against James Ford Seale, charging him with two counts of kidnapping and one count of conspiracy. The following day Seale appeared before United States magistrate Linda Anderson, dressed in prison orange and bound in shackles. He pleaded not guilty. Anderson denied bond, saying, "Neither the weight of the crime nor its circumstance have been diminished by the passage of time."

Representing the government in the trial were Dunn Lampton, United States Attorney for the Southern District of Mississippi; Eric Gibson of the Department of Justice; and Paige Fitzgerald of the Department of Justice. Representing Seale were Kathy Nester and George Lucas, both lawyers with the Federal Public Defender Office in Jackson.

During the opening of the trial in June 2007, prosecutor Paige Fitzgerald of the civil rights division of the Justice Department called to the witness stand Roland Mitchell, a deputy sheriff from Madison Parish Louisiana. At the time of the killings, Mitchell testified that he was among those who went out to the old Mississippi River near Tallulah in 1964, when the lower torso of a human body was found snagged on a branch. It was interesting because Mitchell had a video footage from that day of a young officer wearing a cowboy hat commenting on finding the body. Mitchell testified that an Alcorn A&M College key was found on the body, along with a belt buckle with the initial "M." Moore had been a student at Alcorn.

John Rogan, who worked for the funeral home in Tallulah and who helped recover the body, testified that the legs of the torso were bound together with bailing wire. Renford Williams, another member of the body recovery team, testified how a man and a woman who were out fishing in the backwaters had spotted the remains.

Of course, the key witness was Charles Marcus Edwards, a former Klansman who had admitted helping beat Moore and Dee in the Homochitto National Forest. One of the main things that we learned early on was that Seale was concerned over Charles Edwards having a conscious. That's why he moved Edwards closer to him. He always felt that Edwards, if given an opportunity, might let his conscious be his guide and speak out if pressed.

His fears proved prophetic. Casually dressed in a white shirt, he was obviously nervous when he took the witness stand. He spoke slowly, frequently taking long pauses. He explained that he lied when first questioned about the deaths of Dee and Moore because he was afraid of Seale and his gang members. He knew that Seale would kill him and his wife and their children in a heartbeat. He went on to tell the whole sordid story of the kidnapping, about how he rode in the pickup along with three other Klansmen, following Seale's Volkswagen. He recounted how the teens were tied to a tree and whipped with switches until they were bloody.

At the end of his testimony, he asked if he could address the family members present. "I can't undo what was done forty years ago, and I'm sorry for that," he said to them. "And I ask for your forgiveness for my part in that crime. That's exactly what I wanted to say to you."

Once the prosecution rested, the defense began putting on witnesses. They did not have much to work with. Among them was Don Seale, one of James Ford Seale's brothers, who testified that James had "sore spots" on his arms after being arrested in the 1960s. Another witness was a forensic pathologist who testified that it was impossible to determine the cause of death of the victims. The purpose of his testimony was to raise doubts that the teens might have been alive when they were transported across the state line, a requirement of the federal kidnapping law.

If the teens were killed before they were taken across the state line, it would be a state matter and not a federal one. That argument was squashed on cross-examination when prosecutors were successful in getting the witness to agree that there was no logical reason to bind the feet of dead men before dumping them into the river.

I also testified at the trial, providing a perspective on the investigation forty years ago as well as more recently, when I was brought out of retirement to work on the case. The thing that struck me the most while testifying was what I saw when looking at the jurors in the Killen trial in 2005 and what I saw when looking at the jurors in the Seale trial in 2007.

The Seale jury seemed more serious about the proceedings. They took notes. I walked away feeling different than some of the prosecutors who thought there might be a hung jury. That jury renewed my faith in the jury system in Mississippi. They listened to the witnesses—and they *got* it. James Ford Seale was one of the meanest guys you would ever hope to meet.

On the final day of the trial, the courtroom grew exceptionally quiet anticipating the question that they knew would have to be asked. Finally, Judge Wingate directed a question directly at Seale: "Do you elect not to testify?"

Seale rose to his feet and spoke into the microphone. For the first time, the jurors heard his voice.

"Yes, sir," Seale said.

The defense rested, thus setting in motion the closing arguments by both sides. The prosecution went first, with U.S. Attorney Dunn Lampton standing to speak for the first time in the trial. He described Dee and Moore as "well-liked" teenagers who met their deaths in the most horrible way imaginable. He asked the jury to ponder what Moore may have felt as he watched his friend Henry Dee taken out onto the water and then drowned.

How painful and surreal it must have been for him to watch the killers turn around and come back for him, knowing that the remainder of his life could be measured in passing seconds.

Defense attorney Kathy Nester attacked Edwards's testimony, describing him as someone who has been lying "all these years." Fitzgerald made the last argument on behalf of the prosecution, stressing the believability of Edwards's conversion to the truth.

Two hours later the jury returned with a verdict—guilty on all counts.

"I never had to testify at the trial," says Billy Stokes. "The prosecution wanted Jim to testify because you want Jim Ingram to testify. I had about five current agents testify, and some retired agents. But there was only one Jim Ingram.

I asked Billy, 'Why did they want me to testify?"

"Because you are Jim Ingram."

Seven days later, James Ford Seale returned to the courtroom to receive the sentence imposed by Judge Wingate. He was shackled, hands and feet, and dressed in an orange jumpsuit. The judge described the crime as "unspeakable" and said that only "monsters" could inflict it. Then he sentenced Seale to three life terms in prison for his role in the killings.

Those who thought the nightmare was over were stunned the following year when a three-judge panel of the U.S. Fifth Circuit Court of Appeals vacated the conviction on the grounds the statute of limitations had expired. However, despite the ruling, the judges denied his release until a hearing could take place in May 2009. Judge Wingate mercifully allowed Seale, a cancer patient, to serve his sentence in a medical facility, providing Seale with a degree of compassion that he never showed his innocent victims.

On June 5, 2009, the entire panel of the 5th Circuit Court of Appeals ruled on the case in an evenly divided split decision, thereby upholding the district court's decision. The U.S. Supreme Court was asked to review the case but declined. Seale died in 2011 at the age of 76 in a federal prison.

James Ford Seale being led out of courtroom
Photo by Matt Saldana/Jackson Free Press

Jim and Marie Ingram

15

FINAL CHAPTER

The next major cold case I reviewed for the Justice Department was the infamous Poplarville, Mississippi, lynching. In February 1959, a young white married couple—Jimmy Walters, 22, and June, 21—passed through Poplarville, Mississippi, on their way from Bogalusa, Louisiana, to their home in Petal. It was close to midnight. With them was their four-year-old daughter, Debbie Carol. They were about seven miles outside of Lumberton, when their 1949 Dodge clanked and clattered under the hood and came to an abrupt stop at the top of a hill.

Jimmy allowed the car to coast down the hill, where he steered off the highway to the side of the road. He looked under the hood, but saw nothing he could do to restart the car. Faced with remaining with the car to flag down help—not so attractive since there was very little traffic on the highway, especially at night—or hiking into Lumberton to get help, Jimmy chose the latter and left his wife and daughter locked in the car with the windows cracked for fresh air. He predicted the walk into Lumberton and the ride back with help would take about an hour. June was not happy about being left behind with her daughter, but neither did she want to subject herself and her daughter to the long walk into town.

Not long after Jimmy disappeared into the night, about fifteen minutes it later was determined, a Chevy pulled up alongside the seemingly abandoned Dodge. In the car were five black men. One of the men got out of the Chevy and shined a flashlight into the car, bathing June and her daughter in the blinding yellow glow. June could not see who was holding the light. When it went dark she saw nothing as she heard footsteps and a car door slam shut. Then the car was gone.

More than an hour and a half later, June and Debbie Carol were still alone in the car—where was Jimmy? Had he been beaten up or worse? Her imagination was running wild —when they heard a car approach from the rear and stop. A door opened and closed. Moments later there was the face of a black man at the window, followed by a voice: "Do you need help?"

Frightened, June said she did not need help. Her husband would arrive any minute. Thank you anyway.

The man responded by pressing a pistol against the window.

"Unlock the door."

His voice was hard.

"No," June said.

Without speaking another word, the man smashed the glass with the pistol. Then he reached his arm past the broken glass and unlocked the door. For the first time June saw him clearly. He was a black man.

"You better go away. My husband is on his way here."

"You mean that white son of a bitch that's walking up the street?" His voice had an amused lilt to it.

Stunned, June did not respond. Her heart pounded.

The man reached out and pulled the scarf from her neck and wound it around her neck, creating a noose.

"Please don't hurt me!"

"You white trash bitch, I'm going to fuck you."

The man reached inside the car and grabbed her legs and dragged the one hundred pound woman out into the night. Then he struck Debbie Carol with the pistol and pulled her outside. He walked both of them back to his car and told them to get inside. He then drove about a mile away and turned off onto a logging road, where he stopped the car. He pulled Debbie Carol out and walked her around to the rear of the vehicle and told her to stay there.

Then he walked back to the opened door and told June to lie down on her back across the seat of the car. He told her to pull up her dress, after which he ripped off her panties and lowered himself onto her. After raping her, he told her to take Debbie Carol and start walking.

"If you look back, I'll kill both of you."

June did as she was told. By then it was raining.

Once they reached the highway, they started walking toward Lumberton. At one point, they wandered onto the highway and were almost struck by an eighteen-wheeler that slammed on brakes and skidded to the side of the road. The driver opened the door to his cab and asked if they needed help. June cried out, "I've been raped by a nigger—please help me get to Lumberton to my husband."

224

The truck driver assisted them into his cab and drove them to Lumberton, where they found Jimmy at an all-night truck stop, talking on a pay phone. Within minutes, husband and wife were reunited, the sheriff arrived, and June was transported to the local hospital. Twelve hours later, U.S. Army veteran Mack Charles Parker was dragged from his mother's house and driven to the county jail, where he was charged with raping June Walters.

At a line up, without actually seeing him, June identified Parker as the man who had raped her after authorities asked him to repeat the phrase, "You white trash bitch—I'm going to fuck you!" However, when asked to make a positive identification upon viewing the prisoner, she balked: "I can't be positive because I was scared to death and there wasn't much light."

Parker was transported to Jackson and held at the Hinds County Jail until it was time for his trial. Twelve days after he was returned to the Pearl River County Jail, he was dragged by a mob of nearly a dozen hooded men out into the street and forced into the backseat of a car parked on the south side of the courthouse.

"Please, don't kill me!" Parker begged, his anguished voice clearly audible to many townspeople who lived near the court-house.

 In a procession of five cars, Parker was driven to a bridge over the Pearl River and shot twice in the chest with a .38-caliber pistol. His body was weighted with chains and then tossed into the river. Ten days later Parker's body was found in a pile of driftwood. Because the face of the corpse was so distorted, identification had to be made with fingerprints.

Mississippi Governor J. P. Coleman requested an FBI investigation. President Dwight D. Eisenhower responded with a telegram that read: "It is my earnest hope that there will be swift apprehension of the guilty persons. These agents will, of course, continue to provide full facilities to help in any way in this manner."

Poplarville was soon the home of more than forty FBI agents. They opened an office in the small town to facilitate their investigation. The FBI was able to identify all the members of the lynch mob, but since the lynching violated state law and not federal law the names were submitted to Governor Coleman, who held onto the report for several months before turning it over to

Pearl County prosecutor Bill Stewart and District Attorney Vernon Broome.

When time came for the case to be submitted to a grand jury, Broome told the jury he had decided against using the evidence obtained by the FBI. He advised jury members they could call FBI agents to testify if they wanted to, but no one did. The following day the grand jury issued seventeen other indictments requested by Broome, but no one was indicted for Parker's lynching.

Stunned by that development, the U.S. Justice Department announced plans to take the case before a federal grand jury on grounds that Parker's civil rights had been violated by the lynching. The grand jury contained only one African American.

When called before the grand jury, June Walters said she was not absolutely certain that Parker was the man who had raped her. She said that her rapist was older than Parker and had a lower voice than Parker. The jurors asked for a detailed description of the rape, after which one member asked, "You mean you let that nigger fuck you?"

June responded that she had no choice. More hostile questions ensued and she left the jury room in tears. When Jimmy was called to the witness stand, he was asked why he had stayed married to a woman who had participated in sex with a black man. It was a question he ignored.

After hearing all the evidence, the jury foreman returned no indictments against members of the lynch mob. There would be no justice for Mack Charles Parker.

Four years later, Judge Sebe Dale, the federal judge who oversaw the grand jury testimony, was speaking to a civics club in Connecticut on behalf of the Mississippi Sovereignty Commission, when someone asked him if he thought the killers would ever be brought to justice. He responded there would be no need for that since three of the killers already had passed away.

* * *

The Poplarville lynching case was the last cold case I would ever review for the FBI. I pored over the files the bureau submitted to me, but I was able to identify no living person I felt could be prosecuted for the crime. That was a source of deep regret for me, for I desperately wanted to close the books on yet another unresolved civil rights murder case.

We know who the guilty parties are. We've always known. But when you have local officials who refuse to prosecute—and you have a federal grand jury that refuses to issue indictments—that leaves few avenues open for willing prosecutors, especially when the principles are deceased.

After the Poplarville case, I doubted there would be additional files for me to review because I knew I was running out of time. In 2007 I was diagnosed with cancer of the bile duct. I underwent a surgical procedure called the Whipple (technically called a pancreatoduodenectomy) to remove my bile duct, my gallbladder, the first part of my small intestine, and the head of my pancreas, where most tumors occur.

To my sons' surprise, the waiting room at the hospital filled with concerned highway patrolman during my surgery, prompting questions among others in the waiting room about exactly who could be undergoing surgery.

When I awoke, they told me the surgery had been a success and said if I stayed clean of cancer for a year I would be able to beat it. Almost a year to the day of the surgery, I awoke one morning and knew that something was terribly wrong. A trip to my doctor revealed that the cancer had returned. This time the affected organ was my pancreas. I had already undergone one major surgery to remove a tumor. My doctors felt good about my prospects until they discovered that I had a new tumor.

I knew that my co-author had experienced a serious liver disease that had gone into remission and had written a book about it, so I asked him for a copy since he said there was a chapter on liver cancer. The last time I saw him, face to face, was in the parking lot of a small post office, where we met so I could give him the final bundle of interview tapes for this book. To his surprise, I told him I wanted to be a survivor like him. He told me he sincerely hoped that I would be a survivor.

From then on out, it just went from bad to worse. After weeks of excruciating pain behind one of my ears, I finally went to my radiology-oncologist for tests. We had all convinced ourselves that it was nothing more than a severe infection, something that a stout dose of antibiotics would take care of. When the results came back, I went into the doctor's office to discuss it with him. The doctor got right to the point. My pain was caused by a massive tumor in an inoperable location. The outcome was obvious. The cancer had returned and spread throughout my body, even with protracted chemotherapy. Stan recalls me smiling and lowering my head in resignation. There wasn't much choice, was there?

A few days later, I returned with my family to the doctor's office for my weekly blood tests. The young black lady who normally drew my blood took one look at the paperwork she had received and burst into tears. After she left the room, Stan asked me what had happened. He had never seen such an emotional display by a medical technician. It was not a mystery to me.

"Back when I was public service commissioner, her mother got into some serious trouble," I explained. "I was in a position to help her—and I did."

As the cancer spread, the decision was made for me to enter a hospice. In an odd way it was a liberating experience. I had spent my entire life fighting one thing or another. I wanted to fight the cancer, but I knew I could not. I was at the hospice to die. I understood that. Sometimes you just have to turn loose and go with what life throws your way.

While in the hospice, I received a telephone call with my co-author. Most of our relationship had been based on him asking me questions and me giving the answers, but during the last communication I had with him, I had a question of my own.

"Do you know what I want?" I asked.

Knowing that I was talking about this book, he answered, "Yes, I do—the book will be exactly as you asked for it to be."

I had never thought much about writing a book. But when my sons saw other books published on subjects that I am knowledgeable about, they said, "Dad, you need to do your own book and give your take on events that are part of American history."

As the guest of honor in my room at the hospice, I received a constant stream of visitors. I spent time with my wife and with my three sons, and I asked to spend time with each of the grandchildren, one at a time: Wesley, Brannon, Bethany, Stephanie, Russell, Michelle, Elliott, and James. I wanted to look each of them in the eye to reassure them of my love for them. I wanted them to know that I would always be with them in spirit.

Jim and Marie, center, with family

After my visit with my granddaughter, Bethany, I subsequently received a letter from her that brought tears to my eyes.

> Dear Grandpa,
> I just wanted to write you a note to say thank you for the ways that you have affected my life.
> I think my favorite thing about you, Grandpa, is the way you see people. You don't see social status, race, education, or occupation, but you really appreciate each person as they are. I have watched you treat each person that crossed your path as a friend, not just as a means to an end or a way to get your needs met. I so badly want to see people like this. You are a man of generosity and compassion. This is the Godly legacy that you are leaving behind. You see and treat people as God does. You make people feel loved, appreciated, and so special. Thank you for being an example of this in my life.
> I have loved these past few days with you, Grandpa. I love your sense of humor and the way you still bring so much joy to a room. Most of all, I have loved seeing the way you are clinging to God. He is so real to you right now. I want to live my life in a way that God is real—living, breathing, active in my everyday life. I have you as an example of this.
> Grandpa, you have blessed my life in more ways than you can imagine. I wanted to tell you how I will always remember you—as a man who loved people well. This is the legacy that I want. So, thank you again for being that example for me.
> I love you!
> Bethany

My visitors were not limited to family members. Also coming by to see me were former co-workers, ranging from current and former police officers, highway patrolmen, FBI agents, and former Deposit Guaranty employees. That list also included former members of the Ku Klux Klan, individuals I had hunted down, along with witnesses who had testified at my request at the cold-case murder prosecutions in the 2000s.

One day an older gentleman came by to see me. When I saw who it was I asked my sons to leave the room so that we could talk in private. Later, when they returned, they were naturally curious about the visitor. Asked about his identity, I responded, "Oh, he was just an old Kluker who came by to say bye." And so it went.

Families came and went in the hospice. Most stays seemed to be less than a week. The Ingram family grieved with them and then watched as their loved one passed away and the room was prepared for the next visitor. Families moved in, then moved out. Yet I endured, day after day. At one point, I asked my namesake to pray for the Lord to take me. My sons knew the implications of that, but as much as they loved, respected and admired their father, they couldn't intervene in what they believed to be God's decision.

During the last few days they told me my breathing became irregular while I slept. During my lucid moments, I'd take a breath—and then hold onto it for what seemed an eternity—only to release it with a gasp, much like a swimmer emerging from an underwater swim. This repeated during the night, over and over again, with my family feeling that each deep breath would be my last. This is the point in the narrative where my story comes to an end. Five days before it happened, I received a letter from FBI Director Robert S. Mueller. In the letter, he said he was saddened to learn of my illness. He went on to write:

> I want you to know that your friends in the FBI are keeping you and your family in our thoughts and prayers. As you know, the FBI celebrated a milestone last year—its 100th birthday. The strength of this agency always has been, and remains, its personnel. As we embark on the FBI's second century, you can be assured that those of us in today's Bureau are ever mindful of the enduring legacy of accomplishment left us by its previous generations of employees. For 30 years you served the American people faithfully as a member of this Bureau, holding numerous important positions nationwide and here at FBI Headquarters. I want to extend to you my gratitude for the role that you played in establishing the heritage of this organization.

* * *

Several days after slipping into a coma, Jim took his last breath surrounded by his family. There were no last words. Just a gentle surrender to what he knew was inevitable. Jim had spent the night with him, relieved that morning by Steve who telephoned the others when the end finally came.

"When we took Dad to Hospice, I don't think any of us understood what we were about to endure," Jim later recalled. "We had the choice of home care or hospice, but with Mom's Alzheimer's condition worsening, home care wasn't an option. Those were three very hard weeks on the family. Steve, Stan and I took turns staying with Dad around the clock, in eight to ten hour shifts. The care he received at the hospice was incredible, but we knew we needed to be there for him. Mom was there every day. I don't think she grasped the situation at hand . . . He was coherent enough to know what was happening, and I could tell it was very painful for him."

Billy Stokes was devastated by Jim's death. His job was no longer the same without Jim working cases with him. So he thought about it a while and then turned in his FBI identification badge and retired.

"Jim was fearless. He was willing to take on the liability of everything that happened in a case, good or bad. Give him a case and he will run with it. That is one of the main reasons why he was a go-to guy. I'm not sure Jim Ingram was afraid of anything. Certainly, he was not afraid of his job. I was always conservative. Jim was always willing to push the envelope. I'd say to him, "We have more rules now than when you were a working agent. There have been a couple of hundred rules added on since you retired. All the agents in the office loved the guy."

Stokes thought a minute, his glistening eyes reflecting a combination of grief and awe over a man, the likes of which only comes around every generation or so. Finally, the veteran agent added, "Jim was not the FBI. He was bigger than the FBI."